Fire and Brimstone

- From heaven, in the burning of Sodom and Gomorrah formerly
- From earth, in the burning of Mount Etna lately
- In hell, to burn the wicked eternally

with

The Only Deliverer from Wrath to Come
or, the way to escape the horrible and
eternal burnings of hell

and

Godliness in Principle and Conversation
a necessary preparative to the world's
dissolution and the escaping of
future burnings

by **Thomas Vincent**
Minister of Magdalene, Milk Street, London

Edited by Rev. Don Kistler

Soli Deo Gloria Publications
. . . for instruction in righteousness . . .

Soli Deo Gloria Publications
P.O. Box 451, Morgan, PA 15064
(412) 221-1901/FAX 221-1902

*

*

ISBN 1-57358-089-9

Contents

Fire and Brimstone

Contents

To the Reader

The occasion of my writing these few sheets concerning these three great burnings was the breaking forth of such flames and streams of fire last year at the mouth and sides of Etna, or Mount Gibel. I was willing to take hold of any occasion, especially so suitable as this, to awaken sinners so that they might endeavor to escape from the future and everlasting burnings of hell. And this I thought the rather to do because in the relation given us of those stupendous burnings of Etna, the hand of the Lord was not in the least minded; His name was not once mentioned, and no spiritual applications were attempted by those who drew up the narrative. This, to me, seemed a shame, and quickened me (when others who might have done it better were silent) in my endeavors to make some advantage of this providence for the good of souls.

The chief part of what I have drawn up was several months later, which I purposed to preach upon in the course of my ministry as an appendix to the doctrine of contrition; but, being diverted from that subject by some more severe and threatening providences, I looked upon myself as called at that time rather to preach upon such subjects as might tend to the support of God's people under those sufferings which they were likely to undergo if they would persevere in His ways.

Thus my papers were laid aside and laid asleep. I

thought to bury them in my closet and never suffer them to come forth into the light. But since the fires which have broken forth of late in the city and suburbs of London, as well as Southwark, and the general impression of fear of fire upon the spirits of the inhabitants of London, I thought it might be seasonable at this time to treat the subject of burnings of their houses here (for the preventing of which all diligence should be used); yet that they would above all things endeavor to escape the burning of their persons in the everlasting flames of hell.

If this little book is made use of by the Lord to keep any of you out of hell, give God all the praise, and be mindful at the throne of grace of him who prays for the salvation of all your souls,

Thomas Vincent

Fire and Brimstone

Part One: From Heaven in the Burning of Sodom and Gomorrah

Chapter 1

"Upon the wicked He shall rain snares, fire and brimstone, and an horrible tempest; this shall be the portion of their cup." Psalm 11:6

The Text Opened and a General Doctrine Observed

The Lord is known by the judgment which He executes, whereby He causes sinners to understand even in this world that, as He is patient and long-suffering, merciful and gracious, and ready to be reconciled, so He is holy and jealous, just and righteous, and can be angry, and express His anger in furious rebukes, when He is exceedingly provoked thereunto by sin. And as the anger of the Lord, in the height and fierceness of it, is compared to fire, to a flaming fire which devours round about (Lamentations 2:3), so His most dreadful judgments, the expressions of His anger, are by fire, especially by fire mingled with brimstone. Such showers of fire and brimstone God threatens to rain upon the wicked in our text: "Upon the wicked He shall rain snares, fire and brimstone, and an horrible tempest; this shall be the portion of their cup."

In this psalm is set forth, first, the hatred and indignation of the wicked towards the righteous, which is expressed both in their scoffing at them and their preparing the bow and arrow to shoot at and destroy them (verses 1–2).

The second thing set forth is the hatred and indignation of God towards the wicked, which is expressed in His threatening to rain snares, fire and brimstone, and a horrible tempest upon them to devour them (verses 5–6: "upon the wicked"), that is, upon all the wicked who go on still in their trespasses, especially such as are haters and persecutors of the righteous.

"He shall rain snares." That is, God will entangle and hold them so fast, even like birds under the snares and nets of the fowler, that they shall not be able to flee from and escape the destruction which He will bring upon them.

"Fire and brimstone, and an horrible tempest." No tempest is more horrible than a tempest of fire and brimstone, which God will rain on the wicked. This is an allusion to the real fire and brimstone, miraculously created by God and rained down from heaven upon the wicked cities of Sodom and Gomorrah. Something like this God threatens in His destruction of other places. Isaiah 13:19: "And Babylon, the glory of kingdoms, the beauty of the Chaldees' excellency, shall be as when God overthrew Sodom and Gomorrah." Amos 4:11: "I have overthrown some of you, as God overthrew Sodom and Gomorrah."

And if the wicked escape real fire and brimstone,

and any temporal judgment like it on earth, be sure the Lord will rain a horrible tempest of fire and brimstone upon them in hell.

"This shall be the portion of their cup." The Lord has reserved a portion and prepared a cup for all the children of men. He has a portion of good things for the righteous, and He will give them the cup of blessing and salvation; but He has laid up a portion of evil things for the wicked, and will put into their hands the cup of His wrath and curse. He has reserved ruin and destruction for them by fire and brimstone.

DOCTRINE: God threatens to rain a horrible tempest of fire and brimstone on the wicked as their deserved portion.

I shall not here speak concerning all the dreadful temporal judgments of God upon the wicked, which may be similar to destruction by fire and brimstone. But I shall treat fire and brimstone itself, and the destructions of it, both what has been and what shall be.

My chief design is, as the Lord shall enable, to set forth God's vengeance on the wicked, which shall be hereafter by eternal fire and brimstone in hell, in order to awaken sleepy sinners out of their carnal security. There is no greater awakening consideration in the whole Christian religion than this of the certain danger which all unbelieving sinners are in of hell fire, and because such as are most concerned in the danger are hardly brought to conceive, but most hardly induced to consider this fire, it being so far removed at present from sense. Therefore, by way of introduction to the discourse concerning the burning of hell, I shall first treat the fire and brimstone which was formerly rained from heaven upon the wicked cities of Sodom and Gomorrah, and, second, the fire and brimstone which more lately issued forth from the bowels of the earth in last year's eruption of Mt. Etna, that hereby I may both facilitate the conception and entice persons unto the consideration of the fire and brimstone in hell which eternally shall burn the wicked, whose portion that dreadful place is appointed to be.

Chapter 2

*A Historical Introduction to
the Judgment of Sodom*

Dreadful were the showers of fire and brimstone which came down from heaven upon the wicked cities of Sodom and Gomorrah, Admah and Zeboim. The history of those we have recorded in the Scriptures (the most ancient and certain of all histories) where only this record is originally to be found. But before I speak of this judgment, I shall give the historical introduction, showing what the Scripture relates concerning the places and people, and some transactions before its last ruin and desolation by fire from heaven.

The first notice we have of Sodom is in Genesis 13. It was in the early years of the world that Sodom flourished. The sinners of Sodom were contemporary with Abraham, the father of the faithful; none was like Abraham upon the earth for goodness, and none were like the Sodomites upon the earth for wickedness. The text says that they were sinners before the Lord exceedingly (verse 13). We read that Abraham had, upon the call of God, forsaken his father's house and kindred and come into Canaan with Lot, his brother Haran's son, who sojourned together for a while in the land which God promised to give unto the posterity of Abraham for a possession. Here the wealth and substance, the flocks and herds both of Abraham and Lot, through God's blessings, were greatly increased, insomuch as they could no longer live well together because of the abundance of their cattle and some strife which arose between their herdsmen.

Because of this, Abraham, that all occasions of contention might be avoided, desired Lot to divide and separate himself with his cattle and choose either the right hand or the left. Abraham would take the way that Lot refused. Lot complied with this motion and reasonable proposition, and, lifting up his eyes, beheld that the plains of Jordan were well watered, even as the garden of the Lord. Therefore, making choice of these plains for his cattle, he journeyed eastward towards Sodom, one of the cities of the plains, where he took up his habitation.

It was not long after Lot's sojourning in the wicked city of Sodom that wars broke forth and that city was invaded by four great kings: Amraphel, Arioch, Chedorlaomer, and Tidal, because of their rebellion against Chedorlaomer whom they had served twelve years before. The history of these wars was the event spoken of in Genesis 14. Against the army of these four kings were gathered together the five kings of the cities of the plain and their people, who joined together in battle with their enemies in the vale of Siddim. But the four kings were too mighty for the five and, smiting them, obtained victory over them. Whether the army of the four kings was too numerous, or more warlike and expert in battle, or whether the guilt of the people under the five kings weakened their hands and enfeebled their spirits, it is not said. But this we may reasonably judge: their sins were the cause of their overthrow, and God hereby warned them to repent and turn from the evil of their doings lest a worse evil should overtake and utterly destroy them.

The four kings, having conquered and dispersed the army of the five kings, sacked the cities of Sodom and Gomorrah, and, among other captives, took Lot with his goods and departed.

Abraham was notified quickly by one who had escaped these sad tidings of what had befallen Lot. And though he could not muster up so great a force as to match these four great kings in number, yet, because of the great love which he bore for Lot—who for his sake had come forth from among their own kindred into Canaan with him—and being filled with courage, having as little black guilt within to appal his spirit as any man alive, he armed his 318 trained servants and, without any other help (only Aner, Eshcol, and Mamre were confederated with him), he pursued these kings who were laden with their rich booty. In the night when they were drowned with sleep and security, he divided his little company and assaulted them. This taking place so suddenly and unexpectedly, and at such a time when the host of the kings were unprepared, they were struck with dread and amazement. Without any great resistance that we read of, they fled confused before Abraham, who made a great slaughter among them and pursued them to Hobah. Thus Abraham rescued Lot and the other captives out of their enemies' hands, and recovered all the goods which they had taken away.

In Abraham's return with the spoils of these

great kings, the king of Sodom, who had escaped in
the battle, came forth to meet him and made an offer of all the goods which he had recovered, except-
ing only the persons themselves. Abraham would
not accept so much as a thread or a shoelace of what
had before belonged to so wicked a people as the
Sodomites were. He feared, possibly, that such goods
mingled with his own might prove to be like a moth
to them. However, he would not give the king occasion to say, or anyone to think, that Sodom's goods
had made Abraham rich.

It was a wonderful work of God to bring back the
Sodomites from captivity, and to reinstall the king
of Sodom beyond what he could have looked for by
such unlikely means. And it laid a great obligation
upon the Sodomites not only to respect Lot, upon
whose account Abraham had thus ventured himself,
but chiefly to repent of their sins against God, who
had empowered Abraham for this work, and
delivered his and their enemies into his hands. One
such was Melchizedek, King of Salem and priest of
the High God, who came forth to meet Abraham,
acknowledging with praise and thanksgiving how
little the Sodomites answered their obligation either
unto God or man. This appears in Genesis 19, where
their sin and punishment are set forth.

But before this, in Genesis 18, we read that
Abraham, having entertained three angels, afterwards brought them forward on the way which led
towards Sodom. The chief and most honorable of
the angels, being the Son of God, the angel of the
New Covenant, stayed behind the other two angels
who went onwards towards Sodom; he revealed to

Abraham what he was about to do unto Sodom, givng him to understand that the cry of Sodom and Gomorrah was great and their sins exceedingly grievous, and that now he was going down to visit them for their sins. Whether or not he revealed to him what manner of destruction he intended to bring upon them we have no mention, but whatever it was, Abraham was full of fears because of Lot, and therefore interceded with the Lord on behalf of the place, as wicked as it was, to prevent, if possible, the ruin and destruction thereof which was threatened.

Abraham knew of one righteous person, namely Lot, who was there; and he hoped that there might have been others besides him—if not in the city, at least in Lot's family. And therefore he boldly pleaded with the Lord that He would not destroy the righteous with the wicked, because this would not seem just and right for the Judge of all the earth to do. First, he prayed that if fifty righteous persons were found in Sodom the place might be spared for their sakes. The Lord, being very gracious, readily promised that it would be according to his request.

Abraham, having encouragement from one grant, and fearing what the number of righteous persons in Sodom might be, entreated further that if five were wanting from the fifty the place might not be destroyed; and, having obtained his request herein, he does not rest, but proceeds to beg with expressions of low humility that if but forty, and then if but thirty, and then if but twenty, and last of all if but ten righteous persons were found there, the Lord would spare the place for their sakes. Abraham sped through his whole desire, the Lord assuring him that He would not destroy the place if He found so many as ten righteous persons therein. At this point Abraham stopped asking, before the Lord gave any denial unto his suit; and though Abraham did not request it, yet the Lord Himself resolved that not one righteous person would be consumed in the iniquity of the city. And therefore He sent angels there to destroy the place. So they had a commission to save righteous Lot and his family, as we see in Genesis 19.

The two angels were now come in the evening unto Sodom, while Lot, providentially, was sitting in the gate. Seeing them enter, he rose up from his seat and met them, bowed himself toward the ground, and entreated their favor as to be his guests for the night. Through his importunate request (they refused at first), he prevailed with them, and so brought them home to his house where he entertained them with a feast.

They had not been long in Lot's house before the house was beset by the men of the city upon notice of two extraordinary persons who were there; possibly the bodies which those angels had assumed were very beautiful to the eye and full of sparkling luster, being informed by such glorious spirits. This enticed the beastly—or rather worse than beastly—lusts of the Sodomites, and enflamed them with burning desires to commit that filthy sin with them which is not fit to be named. These desires brought the chief part of the city, old and young, from every quarter, to Lot's house. And when they had come, they demanded him to bring forth those men (as they supposed them to be), so that they might satisfy their lusts upon them. Lot looked upon this as such a piece of inhumane and abominable wickedness, to offer such injury unto strangers, that he stood in front of his door and with fair words endeavored to persuade them not to do this wickedness. Yea, he was so desirous of saving his guests from the filthy lusts of the Sodomites that he endeavored to divert them by offering both his virgin daughters to them to be used (or rather misused) by them as they please, so that his guests might be spared.

But the Sodomites were fully bent upon their wickedness and, deafening their ears against his proposal, they pressed in upon Lot and threatened to deal worse with him than with them, attempting to break open his door. The angels, seeing what danger Lot was in among the furious and lustful multitude, put forth their hands and pulled Lot into his house and, putting forth the power the Lord had given them, they smote the Sodomites with blindness so that they could not find the door. Notwithstanding that judgment of blindness upon their bodies, and being pushed forward by their blind and impetuous lusts, they still sought to reach these men.

At this point, the ruin of Sodom was not far off. The angels revealed to Lot who they were, and that they had been sent by the Lord to destroy Sodom and the neighboring cities because of the crying wickedness that was in them. Therefore, inquiring concerning Lot's relations in that city, the angels bade him bring forth all who belonged to his family. Accordingly, Lot went forth and called his sons-in-law, and gave them to understand what he had heard from the angels concerning the near destruction of the city, and therefore warned them to hasten out of that place. But Lot seemed to his sons-in-law as if he had mocked them, and they gave no heed to any of his words.

The day had come that Sodom and Gomorrah must be destroyed. The angels, in the top of the morning, hastened Lot to come forth; and while he lingered they laid hold of his hands, and the hands of his wife and daughters, and (the Lord being merciful to them) brought them forth, bidding him to flee to the mountain, escape for his life, and not look back lest he should be destroyed. His wife, notwithstanding the warning, did exactly that, and was turned into a pillar of salt. Lot, being full of fears, entreated for Zoar; and for his sake the Lord spared that city so that Lot might retire unto it, while He brought destruction upon Sodom and Gomorrah and the other cities of the plain.

Chapter 3

A General Description of Sodom's Judgment,
Together with the Efficient Cause, Which Was
God, and the Meritorious Cause, Sodom's Sins

Being thus led by the thread of the history, we now come to speak of that most tremendous and dreadful judgment which God executed upon Sodom and Gomorrah, namely that horrible tempest of fire and brimstone which the Lord rained down upon those wicked cities for their sins.

You have the relation and description of this in Genesis 19:23–30: "The sun was risen upon the earth when Lot entered into Zoar. Then the Lord rained upon Sodom and Gomorrah brimstone and fire from the Lord out of heaven. And He overthrew those cities, and all the plain, and all the inhabitants of the cities, and that which grew upon the ground. And Abraham got up early in the morning to the place where he stood before the Lord; and he looked toward Sodom and Gomorrah, and toward all the land of the plain, and beheld, and lo, the smoke of the country went up as the smoke of a furnace. And it came to pass when God destroyed the cities of the plain that God remembered Abraham, and sent Lot out of the midst of the overthrow, when He overthrew the cities wherein Lot dwelled."

In treating this subject concerning the burning

of Sodom and Gomorrah with fire and brimstone, I shall speak:

First, of the causes of this judgment.

Second, of the judgment itself.

Third, of persons on whom it was inflicted and how they were affected.

Fourth, of the persons who escaped.

Fifth, of the spectators.

Sixth, of the use and application which we may make of it.

The Causes of This Judgment

The efficient cause of the judgment of Sodom and Gomorrah was the Lord. "Then *the Lord rained* upon Sodom and Gomorrah brimstone and fire *from the Lord* out of heaven." Every judgment whereof there are second causes in nature is from the Lord; but this judgment was miraculous, and therefore the hand of the Lord was in it more immediately. It was beyond the power of any second causes to effect this great thing, and therefore the Lord put forth His own great power and stretched forth His mighty arm so that He might take vengeance on the wicked Sodomites who had so highly provoked Him by their sins. Deuteronomy 29:23: "The Lord overthrew Sodom and Gomorrah, Admah and Zeboim, in His anger and in His wrath."

The Lord heard the cry of Sodom's sins and was wroth; a fire of anger was kindled in His breast and a fury came up into His face. Therefore, girding Himself with His irresistible power, and clothing

Himself with flaming vengeance as with a garment, He came to plead with His ungodly and wicked people for their sins, rendering His rebukes in such a way as never before was heard of. It was the day of the Lord's recompense, the day of His wrath and fierce anger, a day of trouble and distress, of wasting and desolation. It was a day in which the Lord was revealed from heaven in flaming fire to take vengeance upon the Sodomites, whom He punished with a most fearful destruction, devouring those wicked cities by the fire of His jealousy, so that He might make a speedy riddance of all the sinners who dwelled in them. "The Lord rained upon Sodom and Gomorrah brimstone and fire from the Lord out of heaven." By the Lord on earth we are to understand the Son of God, the second most glorious Person in the Trinity. By the Lord in heaven we are to understand the Father, the first Person, who has committed all judgment unto the Son (John 5:22), from whom He received power to execute the appointed vengeance on wicked Sodom.

The meritorious cause of the judgment upon Sodom and Gomorrah was the sins of those wicked cities. When the Lord arises from His place to take vengeance upon a nation, especially in some notable and remarkable judgment, He is first exceedingly provoked hereunto by the sins of those people. Genesis 13:13: "The men of Sodom were wicked, and sinners before the Lord exceedingly." They exceeded all other nations in their sins, and therefore they exceeded all other nations in their punishment. In Genesis 18:20 we read that "the cry of Sodom and Gomorrah was great, and their sin was

very grievous." It was not their prayers which sent up
such a cry unto heaven, no, they were wholly irreli-
gious and ungodly; but it was their sins, like the
blood of Abel which cried from the ground for
vengeance on him who shed it. The cry of Sodom
was so loud that it came up into God's ears, and
would give Him no rest until He came down to punish. Their sin was very grievous, and not only
grievous unto righteous Lot, who was vexed with the
filthy conversation of the wicked (2 Peter 2:7), but it
was most grievous unto the most holy and righteous
God. It was as a heavy load upon Him, grievous and
hard to be borne. It grieved God, as it were, to the
heart; and therefore He eased Himself of the burden
of their sin by allowing it to fall down with a heavy
weight upon themselves so as to crush and destroy
them together.

There are five sins of Sodom spoken of together.
Ezekiel 16:49–50: "Behold, this was the iniquity of
thy sister Sodom: pride, fullness of bread, and abundance of idleness was in her, and in her daughters
[that is, in her neighboring inferior cities], neither
did she strengthen the hand of the poor and needy.
And they were haughty, and committed abomination before Me; therefore I took them away as I saw
good."

The sins were: (1) pride and haughtiness; (2)
fullness of bread; (3) abundance of idleness; (4)
unmercifulness to the poor; and (5) abomination.

The first sin of Sodom was pride and haughtiness. Proverbs 16:18: "Pride goeth before destruction, and a haughty spirit before a fall." The pride
and haughtiness of the Sodomites revealed itself in

their behavior towards Lot (Genesis 19:7–9). Lot was meek and humble; he spoke fairly and kindly: "I pray you, brethren, do not so wickedly." But they were high, rough, and very haughty in their answer: "And they said, 'Stand back,' and they said again, 'This one fellow came in to sojourn, and he will needs be a judge.' "

It is as if they had said, "Pray, who are you who take it upon yourself to speak so to us? Do you know who you are speaking to? You are a bold and sassy fellow to tell us of wickedness. Will you be our judge? Shall we indeed be judged by such a fellow as you? Pray, wait until we choose you and place you in that office. Shall we submit ourselves to be judged by one who is so contemptible? No, no, we will never tolerate that; it is below our birth and breeding to be curbed by anyone, especially by you who are a stranger, and of such a low spirit as dares not join with us in the way and practice of our city. We will deal worse with you than with them. We will make you know that we are your betters, and that we have power in our hands to bring you to your knees and tread you under our feet. We can do with you and yours what we please. We have been often provoked by you before; now we will forbear no longer, but will make you feel as well as see in what disdain we have taken all your proofs of our conduct."

Pride had grown to a great height in Sodom. It was monstrously great and big-bellied, conceiving and bringing forth many daughters: hatred, malice, envy, revenge, wrath, strife, contention, bitterness, evil speaking, slanders, backbiting, whisperings, tumults, brawls, blood, and the like. These and many other sins are the product of pride and haughtiness, all which we have good reason to think exceedingly abounded in these exceedingly wicked cities of Sodom and Gomorrah.

The second sin of Sodom was fullness of bread. By bread we are to understand all sorts of food, and not only meat, but drink too. Matthew 6:11: "Give us this day our daily bread." By fullness of bread is not meant plenty of food, this being God's gift; and no man sins who would have it and make use of it moderately. But hereby we are to understand the Sodomites' filling themselves: their excessive eating to the point of gluttony and excessive drinking to the point of drunkenness. They pampered the flesh, and nourished themselves as the ox is nourished against the day of slaughter. Some resemblance of their sin was spoken of the Israelites in Amos 6:4–6: "That lie upon beds of ivory, and stretch themselves on their couches, and eat the lambs out of the flock, and calves out of the midst of the stall; that chant to the sound of the viol, that drink wine in bowls, and anointed themselves with the chief ointment."

They were such as those against whom the woe is pronounced in Isaiah 5:11–12: "Woe unto them that rise up early in the morning, that they may follow strong drink, and continue until night, till wine enflames them; and the harp and the viol, the tabret and pipe and wine are in the feasts; but they regard not the work of the Lord, neither consider the operations of His hands." It is likely that the Sodomites had been feasting and reveling, drinking and carousing that day when the angels came into their city. And so the Sodomites, having their lusts

enflamed with their excesses, gathered in troops at
the house of Lot to commit their intended outrage.
But God was so provoked that He cut off all
provisions for the flesh, which they had greatly
abused, and cut them off too for their intemperance.

The third sin of Sodom was abundance of idleness. Idle persons abounded in that city. They sat
down to eat and drink, and rose up to play; they were
busy and active indeed in the service of the devil, but
either they lived without any particular calling,
many of them, or were very slothful and negligent
therein. Had they been diligently employed in their
callings that day when the angels visited Lot, they
would have had more mind to stay in their own
houses than to disturb strangers in another's house.
But being so generally idle, and an idle crew of
them going together upon notice that the strangers
were being entertained in Lot's house, for want of
better employment, they attempted this wickedness.
The Sodomites not only wasted their wealth and
strength, but also their precious time in luxury; and
this provoked the Lord to put an end to their time,
of which they themselves made so little account.

The fourth sin of Sodom was being unmerciful
to the poor. They did not strengthen the hands of
the poor and needy; they had poor and needy persons among them, but they neither strengthened
their hands nor comforted their hearts by giving relief. They consumed so much upon their lusts that
they had nothing to spare for the poor; at least they
had no heart to give anything for the supply of their
necessities. The cry of the poor, most likely, with
their other sins, came up into God's ears. And in

James 2:13 the Lord has threatened, "He shall have judgment without mercy that hath shown no mercy."

The fifth and chief sin of Sodom was abomination. "And they committed abomination before Me; therefore I took them away as I saw good." This word "abomination" is a general word, and may be attributed to the aforementioned sins, which are an abomination in the sight of God. But ordinarily it is attributed in Scripture to the greatest and most heinous sins, and among others, yea, above others, to the sin of idolatry. The Sodomites, no doubt, were guilty of this sin; however, it is not made mention of, neither do I think that sin is implied in the word "abomination" here insomuch as then the earth was full of idolatry, and the Sodomites were no worse herein (as we read) than other nations. Rather, I conceive that, by "abomination," we are to understand the abominable filthiness of the Sodomites, for which they are branded by the apostle. Jude 7: "Even as Sodom and Gomorrah, and the cities about them in like manner, giving themselves over to fornication, and going after strange flesh, are set forth for an example." They gave themselves over to fornication, even as the Gentiles are said to do. Ephesians 4:19: "Who being past feeling have given themselves over unto lasciviousness, to work all uncleanness with greediness." God had given them up, and they had given themselves up to the service of their lusts. They were generally addicted to uncleanness, and not only to fornication and adultery, but it is said that they lusted after "strange flesh," such was their lust and uncleanness. We have it described in Romans 1:24–27, which tells that they dishonored their own bodies among themselves, the men through vile affections, leaving the natural use of the woman; how they burned in their lusts towards one another, men with men working that which is not only unseemly to be practiced, but also unseemly to be named or, more particularly, described. The sin, since that time, has obtained the name of "sodomy," it being so general in that place insomuch as, when the angels came to Sodom, they would have been unclean with the very angels. This provoked the Lord to render to them the recompense for such abominable filthiness as was fitting.

Besides the sins of the Sodomites, we may collect from history several aggravations of their sins, which exceedingly ripened them for ruin.

The first aggravation of the Sodomites' sin was their impenitence. Although Nineveh was threatened with ruin, and that within forty days, yet upon their repentance at the preaching of Jonah, God repented of the evil threatened and did not destroy them, as we read in the book of Jonah. And if Sodom had repented of their sins and turned from their evil ways, if they had washed and made themselves clean, and put away the evil of their doings from before God's eyes, God would have turned from the fierceness of His displeasure, and though their sins were of a scarlet and crimson dye, yet they would have been blotted out and washed away, made like snow or wool. But this was the aggravation of all their other wickedness, that they were insensible and hard-hearted; their consciences were seared as with a hot iron, so that they had no feeling of remorse.

There was a preacher of righteousness among then, namely righteous Lot, who reproved them so plainly and roundly for these ungodly practices and filthy conduct that they told him he was trying to make himself a judge by his own blameless conversation and forbearance from such intemperance and riot as they ran to. But the Sodomites deafened their ears against Lot's reproofs, and would not be led by any of his example. Nothing prevailed with them to repent.

The second aggravation of the Sodomites' sins was their incorrigibleness. As was said of the Jews in Jeremiah 5:3, so it might have been said of the Sodomites then: "Though God had stricken them, yet they did not grieve; though God had consumed them, yet they refused to receive correction." They did not take warning by lesser judgments so as to be corrected and amended thereby. They were smitten before their enemies; their city had not long before been sacked, their goods taken away, and they themselves were led into captivity with their wives and children, yet they were insensible of their sins, the cause of all this evil that came upon them. And they were so far from being bettered hereby that they grew worse than they were before!

The third aggravation of the Sodomites' sin was their ingratitude. They were not only ungrateful to Lot—upon whose account Abraham delivered them out of the hands of their enemies, which laid an obligation of respect to Lot upon them as long as they lived—but chiefly they were ungrateful to God, the Author of this deliverance by Abraham, and who, moreover, had been very bountiful to them in giving them such a place of plenty and pleasure. It was like the garden of the Lord for fruitfulness. The greater God's mercy and bounty to them was, the greater was their ingratitude, and the more highly aggravated were their sins.

The fourth aggravation of the Sodomites' sin was the universality of their sins. There were no righteous persons among them, unless it was Lot and his family. The Sodomites were generally corrupt; they were all dross and no gold, all water and no wine, totally wicked once Lot had departed. As the earth of old was filled with violence, so Sodom then was filled with filthiness, which was very offensive to the pure and holy eyes of God, and provoked Him to destroy them.

The fifth aggravation of the Sodomites' sins was their shamelessness. What was said of Israel in Jeremiah 6:15 might have been said of Sodom: "Were they ashamed when they had committed abominations? Nay, they were not at all ashamed, neither could they blush." When Isaiah wanted to set forth the shamelessness of Judah's sins, he compared them to Sodom. Isaiah 3:9: "The show of their countenance doth witness against them; they declare their sin like Sodom; they hide it not." None had more reason to blush and be ashamed than such filthy sinners as they, and yet none were less ashamed! Instead of being ashamed of their sins, they gloried in their shame.

The sixth aggravation of the Sodomites' sins was their security. They ate, they drank, they bought, they sold, they planted, they built, until judgment overtook them (Luke 17:28). They were generally secure, though they had sinned so greatly and, by their sins, highly provoked the Lord to take vengeance upon them. They put the evil day far from them. Lot's sons-in-law, although foretold and forewarned by their father, would not believe it was so near, much less did the rest of the Sodomites believe any such thing who had no intimation thereof given to them. They gave little thought to what a day would bring forth; their impunity increased their security for a while, and their security, under the guilt of such heaven-daring sins, aggravated their sin exceedingly.

And now the lusts of the Sodomites, having conceived and brought forth such sins, and their sins being so aggravated, arrive unto perfection and bring forth death. Their iniquities are now full, and the vials of God's wrath also are full; and He poured them down upon their heads. This leads to the next particular, to speak of the judgment itself inflicted upon Sodom and Gomorrah.

Chapter 4

A Particular Description of Sodom and Gomorrah's Burning by Fire and Brimstone From Heaven

This chapter concerns the judgment itself which was inflicted upon Sodom and Gomorrah. It was fire and brimstone which was rained down from heaven upon those cities. The morning was clear when Lot went forth from Sodom; and the sun had risen when he entered into Zoar. But then a strange darkness quickly filled the face of the heavens and hid the sun from view. We may conceive that the fashion of the heaven was altered, and that the clouds which carried this horrible tempest of fire and brimstone were of another shape than those which carry ordinary storms of rain or hail, of thunder and lightning.

It was over Sodom and Gomorrah that these dreadful clouds were gathered, which, upon the command of the Lord, broke asunder; and it is likely that it was with fearful lightning accompanied with great cracks and amazing noise, as if heaven and earth and hell had been coming together. The clouds let down these flaming showers, which strangely turned the air into fire, and with such irresistible violence beat upon the houses of the Sodomites that they were forced to yield unto the fury of these devouring flames.

This rain was probably not in small drops, like
that which falls upon the tender grass and causes it
to spring forth and flourish; but it was in great
flakes of scalding sulphurous matter kindled by the
breath of God. It is likely that great sheets of fire
came down from heaven, like the flying roll spoken
of in Zechariah 5:2–4: "The length thereof was
twenty cubits, and the breadth thereof ten cubits,
which entered into the house of the thief and false
swearer, and consumed the timber thereof, and the
stones thereof." So did these sheets and rolls of fire
fly about the cities of Sodom and Gomorrah, and entered into the houses of the unjust and profane, the
filthy and unclean, smiting and consuming inhabitants with their habitations.

This storm of fire and brimstone, coming down
with a commission from God to destroy the whole
place, armed itself with inexpressible rage and fury,
and, first smiting the heads and tops of all the
houses in the city, set them on fire together. This
mounted a great flame upward, and that, mingling
with the sulphurous fire which came downward, was
exceedingly the more enraged. We may conceive
that from here came such horrid blazes to the eye,
and such dreadful roarings to the ear, as awakened
all the wicked inhabitants of the city out of their
sleep and security, and filled them with inconceivable horror and perplexity, when they saw inevitable
ruin so near.

Then the streets of the city were filled with
flames, and the rain from heaven likely raised floods
and streams of burning brimstone which poured
into the houses on every side such fire as no water

could quench, no stone walls or iron bars or gate could resist or defend any of the inhabitants from being devoured thereby. Thus God's hand found out all His enemies in these wicked cities. His right hand laid hold of those who hated Him and took no heed to His laws; and, making Sodom and Gomorrah as a fiery oven in the time of His anger, He swallowed up all the sinners of those places in His wrath, and devoured them with this unquenchable fire. The place became like a fiery oven or a great fiery furnace, the smoke of whose flame was so great that far and near it might be seen.

Concerning the horror of the Sodomites when compassed about with flames, I shall speak more under the third particular. Here I shall only add the things which were remarkable in this judgment: first, the strangeness of it; second, the suddenness and unexpectedness of it; and, third, the dreadfulness of it.

First, this judgment was very strange. It is the nature of fire to ascend towards heaven, but here fire and brimstone descend together from heaven—this is very strange. The Sodomites had an unnatural fire within them, and they have an unnatural fire sent upon them. They lusted after strange flesh (Jude 7), and God punished them with strange fire. Job 31:3: "Is not destruction to the wicked, and a strange punishment unto the workers of iniquity?"

But of all strange punishments, this is one of the most strange; never such a thing was heard of before or has been known since. I may apply what Moses said on another occasion in Deuteronomy 4:32: "Ask now of the days that are past, which were before thee, since God created man upon the earth, and ask from one side of heaven unto the other, whether there hath been such a thing as this great thing, or hath been heard like it," that God should rain fire and brimstone from heaven to punish wicked cities.

We read of fire sent down from heaven by the Lord upon Elijah's request, which consumed his sacrifice, even though he had drenched it often and surrounded it with water, all of which was licked up by the fire to the wonder and astonishment of the people. Hereby the Lord revealed His power beyond Baal's, whose priests could not by all their prayers and cutting themselves prevail with their god to effect any such thing (1 Kings 18:26–39). We also read of fire sent down from heaven which destroyed two captains and their fifties, upon the request of the same prophet. These things were exceedingly strange. But the rain of fire and brimstone which consumed several cities, and all their inhabitants together, was far more strange. Fire has come from heaven, but never such great fire. Fire has come down from heaven, but never fire mingled with brimstone. Fire and brimstone have come forth from the bowels of the earth (of which I will treat in the second discourse of this book), but never did fire and brimstone come down from heaven, either before or since.

Second, this judgment was sudden and unexpected. It was like the flood to the old world, which was drowned, or like the coming of Christ to the sinners on earth, who shall be damned. When the greatest judgments are nearest, the sinners who shall be destroyed thereby are most secure. And thus it was with the sinners of Sodom. The day before there was no appearance of any such destruction near; there was no sign in the earth or in the heavens of any such thing. The night before was like other nights: no fire beginning in any place, only the fire of lust which burned and raged in the hearts of that wicked people; but they had no apprehension of danger from those flames. When the morning came it was like other mornings: there were no fiery dews or drops of fiery rain to give them a warning of what would follow.

The shadows of night were chased away by the beams of the morning sun. There was no appearance of the shadows of the night of death ready to stretch forth themselves upon all the inhabitants of Sodom and the neighboring cities. But as soon as Lot had entered into Zoar, the Lord rained fire and brimstone on Sodom and Gomorrah, and brought such a sudden destruction upon them as they could not escape. Even so will it be ere long with Babylon (Revelation 18:7–8). And so it was with Sodom: she lived deliciously and securely, and in one day death and mourning came upon her, and she was utterly burned with fire.

Could the Sodomites have foreseen and foreknown what destruction would have befallen their city that day, they would have hastened out of the place the day before; at least they would have delayed no longer than that morning when Lot departed. They would have flocked about him, young and old from every quarter, and would have departed with him. They would not have valued houses or goods, but saved only their lives.

But the Sodomites did not in the least apprehend their destruction to be so near. The angels knew it, but they revealed it only to Lot. If they had made it known to the Sodomites, most likely they would not have believed it any more than Lot's sons-in-law believed Lot when he declared it. The Sodomites were jovial and secure, as if their life and mirth would continue for many years, when neither their life nor their mirth was to continue a day longer.

Third, this judgment was most dreadful. We read in Scripture, and have seen with our eyes, very great judgments; but none is so dreadful, all things considered, as this of fire and brimstone from heaven. Indeed, the flood which devoured the whole earth (except Noah and his family) struck the most universal dread upon the children of men of any judgment that ever has been since the world's creation; yet the fire and brimstone which devoured Sodom and Gomorrah with all their inhabitants (only Lot and his family excepted) had more of particular dread in it inasmuch as death by fire is more painful than death by water—especially such fire as came down from heaven.

It was a terrible day to the old world when they saw the windows of heaven opened and water coming forth from there in such great abundance as to swell into a flood, and that so great a flood as drowned all mankind who were not found in the ark. But it was a more terrible day to the Sodomites when they saw the windows of heaven opened and fire coming forth from there—fire mingled with brimstone, and God's fiery indignation. This fell on their houses and heads; it put all into flames. This last judgment, as it had more strangeness in it, so it struck more terror into the hearts of those who endured it.

When the ground was cleaved asunder and the earth opened her mouth and swallowed up Korah, Dathan, and Abiram, with all that appertained to them; when they went down alive into the pit and the earth closed upon them again, they perished from the congregation (Numbers 16:32–33). This was a very fearful judgment, but the opening of the heavens, and their showering down fire and brimstone, which swallowed up Sodom and Gomorrah and all the sinners therein, was far more fearful. Death by sword, death by pestilence, or by any other disease has nothing of that dread in it as death by fire, especially fire from heaven mingled with brimstone.

No fire that we have ever seen carried so much dread in it as the fire that burned down our city of London; but London's fire was nothing in comparison to Sodom's fire. This will appear if we compare them together.

The fire of London began in only one place, which awakened all the inhabitants around to prepare and secure themselves and their goods; but the fire of Sodom began in all places together. There was fire outside the city and fire within; fire in every street and in every house at the same time. The Sodomites were compassed about with fire on all sides.

The fire of London consumed but a part, although it was the greatest part of the city within the walls; but the fire of Sodom consumed the whole city, turned all into ashes, and not one house therein escaped the fury of the flames.

Though the fire of London devoured the houses, yet much of the wealth and best goods of the city were preserved; but Sodom's fire consumed all their wealth: their gold and silver were melted; all their apparel and rich household furniture were burned; and whatever provisions they had made for their flesh, whatever fuel they had laid up for their lusts, became fuel for this fire.

Though the fire of London burned much of the goods as well as the houses, which could not so easily and quickly be removed, yet few, very few of the inhabitants perished. They had time and warning to withdraw themselves before the fire reached so far as their habitations. But Sodom's fire burned persons as well as houses; and not one person in the whole city escaped after the fire had begun. Such as went out of doors were consumed by the fire from heaven; such as remained within were consumed by the fire of their houses.

The fire of London was an earthly fire, although the contriving of it might be first in hell, and hellish instruments made use of in the beginning and carrying on of it; but the fire of Sodom and Gomorrah was from heaven. And if the one expressed more of the wrath of the devil and devilish men, the other expressed more of the wrath of the sin-avenging God, which is ten thousand times more dreadful.

The fire of London was extinguished, since which time the city is being rebuilt, and now lifts up with more beauty and luster than before it was turned into ashes. But Sodom's fire made a desolation of the place, and since the conflagration of that city Sodom never was, and never will be again, rebuilt. Neither is the place capable now of having any building erected upon it inasmuch as the Dead Sea now covers the place wherein the Sodomites had their habitation.

Chapter 5

The Persons Who Were Consumed
and How They Were Affected

The persons were the wicked inhabitants of the cities of Sodom, Gomorrah, Admah, and Zeboim. Great was the horror (hinted at before) which we may imagine these persons were in when the fire and brimstone came down from heaven upon them and there was no way for them to escape.

We may conclude that the noise and scorching heat of this dreadful fire quickly awakened some out of their sleep of intemperance, and all out of their sleep of security. What tongue can utter the horrible perplexity of the Sodomites on this day when they opened their doors and windows in the morning, and, looking up to heaven, saw them open and rain down fire to devour them; when the tempest of fire and brimstone beat upon them so sorely and suddenly; when there was such a dreadful, burning heat from the fire, and such a stinking, noisome, suffocating smoke from the brimstone; when there was a kind of little hell in that place, both for torment and sin! Oh, the dread of the Sodomites! Oh, the confusion they were in when such an unthought-of, unheard-of, and unavoidable ruin came upon them! How they were amazed! How they were distressed!

Some, it may be, cursed the day of their birth,

wishing that they had been aborted so that they might not have lived to see the light of the sun, so that they might not have lived to see and feel the fire of this day. Others may have cursed themselves, and the sinners there who had provoked God to send this dreadful judgment upon them. Others may have cursed God because of the fire and great heat, like those in Revelation 16:8–9 who, being scorched with great heat, blasphemed the name of God who had sent down the fire upon them.

Oh, what a horrible outcry there was in Sodom when the city began to be in flames! Oh, what weeping and wailing and wringing of hands! The men roar, the women shriek, the children weep and cry and cling to their parents; yea, all of them weep and cry out most hideously.

The Sodomites now have tears in abundance, but none of their tears could quench the flames around them or assuage the sorrow and anguish within them. Tears before this might have prevented these flames, and their fruitless mourning in the midst of them; but none were more impenitent than they in the time of their prosperity, and therefore their cries and tears are to no purpose in the time of their adversity. They weep, and God laughs at their calamity; they are grieved and afflicted, and God is comforted in the execution of His vengeance upon them for their sins.

In this extremity, the Sodomites do not know what to do, nor which way to turn. They dare not go forth to consult one another, because the air is all on fire, and there are streams of fire and brimstone which overflow in the streets. All the shelter they have is for a little while in their houses, but the fire invades them there and hems them in on all sides. Very quickly the fire creeps in at their windows and breaks through their doors; nothing is able to withstand its force.

We may imagine how the poor Sodomites, when the fire was coming into their houses, ran from room to room, being pursued wherever they went by the devouring flames. And when the fire had reached their bodies, and the flames began to seize upon them, first they sweated and then they fried. Their hair was singed; their clothes were set afire; their sinews shrank; their hands and feet lost their use, and they were in horrible pain all over without any help or relief. Refuge failed them and there was no escape, no enduring this pain; and yet they must endure it until the extremity of pain took away all sense of pain.

The terror of the Sodomites, through the apprehension of their present and unavoidable death before them, was great; but surely the way and manner of it, namely by fire from heaven, caused greater terror. If it had been an ordinary fire, to which some natural cause might have been assigned, it would not have been so much; but when it was a miraculous fire from heaven, created on purpose by the Lord to destroy those cities, surely their dread was extraordinary. They could not help but see the more immediate hand of God in it, and, withal, His frown and dreadful displeasure.

With the fire and brimstone which fell down from heaven upon their houses and bodies, they had scalding drops of God's wrath which fell down upon their consciences. We may imagine what impressions they had of the wrath of the sin-avenging God on their spirits, which caused a greater horror within than the bare apprehension of death in any shape could, of itself, effect, when the guilt of such great sins and the apprehensions of such great wrath met together in their consciences, and they had no time or way to get the guilt of sin removed and the wrath of God appeased; when conscience, which was before asleep, was awakened in the midst of flames; when there was a fire above the Sodomites, the fire of God's anger; fire around and upon the Sodomites, the fire which came down from heaven; fire beneath the Sodomites, the fire of hell; and fire within the Sodomites, the fire kindled in their consciences—oh, the horror, when hell was already begun within them in the slashes and sparks of it! Words cannot utter the horrible anguish which then they had upon them!

Chapter 6

The Persons Who Escaped

The persons who escaped this dreadful judgment were Lot and his family. In the old world, Noah was an upright man in his generation, while the rest of the entire world was wicked. And God provided an ark wherein He saved Noah and his family, while all the kindreds and nations of the world besides were drowned in the deluge of water which was brought upon the earth. So also Lot was the only upright and righteous man in Sodom, while all the city, together with the neighboring cities, were wicked. God provided a Zoar for Lot, while He brought a deluge of fire upon those wicked cities, which consumed them, and all the remaining wicked who dwelled in them (2 Peter 5:6–8).

When the destroying angels were sent to Sodom, God remembered righteous Lot, and a mark for preservation was set upon his forehead because he sighed and cried out for the abominations which were committed in the midst of the city. And God remembered Abraham, his friend, who had made intercession for Lot; therefore He sent him out of the midst of the overthrow when He overthrew the city in which Lot dwelled.

Chapter 7

The Spectators at Sodom's Burnings

Abraham, however remote his habitation was, had a plain sight of this fire and the burning of Sodom. Genesis 19:27–28: "And Abraham got up early in the morning unto the place where he stood before the Lord; and he looked toward Sodom and Gomorrah, and toward all the land of the plain, and beheld, and lo, the smoke of the country went up as the smoke of a furnace." Abraham's heart told him that those wicked cities would not escape destruction, whatever conditional promise the Lord had made unto him of their preservation. Therefore, it is likely that he rose and came to this place so that he might see what became of the cities. He quickly perceived them to be in flames by the great smoke which mounted up from them. What his thoughts were is not mentioned, but it is likely that he was more than ordinarily affected with this more-than-ordinary judgment. Such an appearance of God in the world, clothed with such wrath and vengeance, might well make even Abraham himself, whatever interest he had in God, quake and be astonished. When he looked up to heaven, he saw God all in flames of anger; when he looked down to the earth, he saw Sodom and Gomorrah all in flames of fire. He knew that Lot dwelled there, and he did not know but that Lot and

his family might be burning there; and this caused
him to lift up his voice and weep.

Be sure that he knew the wickedness of the
Sodomites to be very great, and that the righteous of
the place were very few, if any, when the Lord had
promised to spare the whole city for the sake of ten
righteous persons, could ten be found. "Ah, Lord,"
he thought, "what a wicked place Sodom is that it
could not yield ten righteous persons!"

What an evil and bitter thing it is to sin against
God, and hereby to provoke Him to anger! What a
fearful thing it is to fall into the hands of the living
God when His anger is stirred up and burns like
fire! And if Abraham could so clearly discern the
burnings of Sodom and Gomorrah, the inhabitants
of Zoar, who dwelled so near, might more clearly
discern it.

They had an alarm in the morning which startled and awakened them. They were called forth out
of their houses to see this dreadful and tremendous
sight. The cries of "Fire, fire, fire" sounded in the
ears: fire from heaven, fire in the air, fire on the
earth, Sodom on fire, Gomorrah on fire, Admah and
Zeboim on fire; every place near them on fire. This
they hear; this they see; the flames all about are very
visible and very terrible. Oh, with what rueful countenances they looked upwards towards heaven, from
whence this fire came, and forward towards Sodom
and Gomorrah, where the fire was kindled! They saw
all the cities together in flames, which, being
situated upon the plain, without any mountain or
hill between, they might, from the fields or the
housetops, have an easy view of.

And surely the sinners of Zoar were now afraid, and fear exceedingly surprised the guilty. Surely their consciences were now awakened and caused a trembling within them when they saw God's vengeance executed in flaming fire upon their fellow sinners before them. "Alas! Woe to us! Who can endure such devouring fire? Who can bear such horrible burnings? Have Sodom and Gomorrah provoked God to destroy them with fire from heaven? What, then, will become of us who have shared in their guilt and deserve the same punishment? Oh, where can we flee to hide us from the wrath of God, and shelter us from His fiery indignation?"

Though Lot did not look back as his wife did, before he got into Zoar, from thence, no doubt, he looked with a sorrowful countenance and a more sorrowful heart upon the wretched cities as they burned, especially on Sodom, the chief city, and where his habitation had been. Oh, the tears that must have run down his cheeks! Oh, the grief that must have filled his heart when he saw such a strange shower of fire and brimstone raining down from heaven upon that sinful—and now woeful—place!

He was vexed at the sins of the Sodomites before, and how he was grieved at their misery. He thought of his sons-in-law and lamented their folly, who, notwithstanding his warning, stayed there to be burned (which he knew they lamented now much more). He thought of this neighbor and that neighbor, how they were weeping and crying while they were melting and frying in the flames.

But Lot did not abide long in Zoar, for such fear,

as well as grief, possessed him that he did not think himself safe there; and therefore he fled to the mountain, where he was warned at first to go by the angels, and there dwelt in a cave with his two daughters (Genesis 19:30).

Chapter 8

Application to the Ungodly

We have set before us an example, and that both of the Sodomites' burning and Lot's escaping. These things are recorded for our example. The former is an example to the ungodly; the latter is an example to the righteous.

The Sodomites' burning is an example to the ungodly. 2 Peter 2:6: "And turning the cities of Sodom and Gomorrah into ashes, God condemned them with an overthrow, making them an example unto those who afterwards should live ungodly."

This example is set forth both to reprove and warn the ungodly. It reproves the ungodly, and that for the practice of such sins as were the cause of Sodom's ruin.

The first is pride and haughtiness. I believe many in our age and nation will vie with any of the Sodomites of old for devilish pride and haughty spirits (if we guess the pride of the heart by the garb, the look, and the speech). There are some, and those not a few, who seem to have outdone all former generations, and may well be called the first-born of the devil for this sin, although they have been brought forth at the latter end of the world.

What shall we say when men of higher rank generally, without need, disguise and hide their heads in others' hair, and that of the womanish length, and for the most part of another color than their own; when women disguise and hide the natural color of their faces with paint and patches? What shall we think of the flaunting apparel, the antique and apish fashions, of the ruffling gallants in our nation? Not to speak of the excessive cost bestowed on their changeable raiment, more being spent upon one suit worn by some but a few days than would be sufficient to clothe the backs and fill the bellies of scores of poor Christians; nor to insist upon the excessive time spent (or, rather, misspent) in dressing, wherein some consume nearly half the time they are awake.

What shall we say of the taunting language, the scornful and reproachful speeches with which some fill their mouths, and which they spit forth upon the people of God, and that because of their holiness and likeness to God, whereby they not only despise them, but the God whose image they bear?

What shall we think of the stately buildings, the excessive shows and flourishes outside, and the expensive furniture within, when houses are newly risen out of the ashes and the church lies waste; when so many poor families are brought to share a morsel of bread? What do these things, with many more which I might mention, signify but that pride compasses such persons about like a chain, whereby they are enthralled and captivated?

And let me say this: the devil has hold of the end of this chain, and is thereby dragging people downwards towards the lowest hell.

And here I could wish that professors of religion

themselves, and many who in other regards fear God, could acquit themselves from the guilt of many gross, outward demonstrations of inward, prevailing pride. I will not say that all who have false hair have false hearts. I know some who are true-hearted and simply lack a covering there. Nor do I say that all who are curious in decking their outside according to fashion are wholly untrimmed and unadorned within. Yet I could wish that the art of wigmaking had never been discovered, and that the ways of the French had never been brought into our nation. And I will say that plain apparel and dress very well become persons of great honor, especially professors of religion; that it is very unsuitable to the times for any to bestow much cost on ornaments when many of Christ's members lack necessities. And it is very unsuitable to the Christian profession to bestow much time on adorning the body when the soul has more need, on the washing and adorning of which the times and pains would be best bestowed. But I move on to the reproof of the ungodly for the rest of Sodom's sins.

Fullness of bread, or intemperance in eating and drinking, was another sin with which Sodom was charged. And how many are there in our days who may be charged with the same, who come behind none in this sin? We read of the prodigal in Luke 15 who wasted his substance with riotous living. If we look abroad, we may find too, too many of these everywhere, whose belly is their god, who pamper the flesh, who indulge and enslave themselves to their appetites, who give themselves permission to exceed all bounds in their riotous practices, spending their

whole time and substance in their profuse living.
See how the apostle set forth riotous persons in
2 Peter 2:12–13.

This reproves excessive drinking, a sin more in
use among us than that of excessive eating. What is
more common than this sin of drunkenness, both
in the city and in the country? How many are there
who guzzle and swill in drink without measure, who
drench and soak themselves with ale and other
strong liquors, who besot and drown their natural
parts and gifts, wasting their time in rambling up
and down to taverns and alehouses, consuming
their wealth, distempering their bodies, and provok-
ing God to destroy their souls! Woe to such persons
(Isaiah 5:11 and 22:13; Proverbs 23:29–30).

Abundance of idleness was the third sin of
Sodom. And when did this sin more prevail than in
our licentious age? Idleness is a constant
companion of intemperance, yea, rather the mother
that brings it forth, at least the nurse that brings it
up. How many golden sands of time do most allow
to run waste? How many golden seasons do they let
slip, wherein they might make provision for
eternity? If they knew the worth of time, especially of
the harvest time, the summer day of the gospel, they
would not lavish their time as they do; they would
not sleep in the harvest and waste the whole day in
idleness; they would not sin until the night of death
overtook them and suddenly surprised them, when
the least minute of time cannot be recalled, though
they could and would give ten thousand worlds for
it.

Unmercifulness to the poor was another of

Sodom's sins which the ungodly are chargeable with here, and shall be charged with and condemned for at the day of Christ's appearance (Matthew 25:41–42). It is no wonder that those who have not pity on their own souls should have their bowels shut up against the poor; that those who spend so much on their lusts should not spare anything for the relief of others' wants. None have more marble bowels than those who have the hardest hearts; and none are more merciful than those who are most ungodly and sinful.

Abominable filthiness is the last and chief sin of the Sodomites. And if the skirts of England were turned up, what filthiness would there appear under them? It is a shame to speak of what is done by some in secret; yea, too many declare their uncleanness like Sodom, and are not ashamed to practice it in the sight of the sun. Whoredom and adultery, what is more common in this debauched generation? Yea, I hope that too many in England, as well as Italy, are not guilty of the sin of Sodom, properly so called (I mean lusting after strange flesh). Such vile affections some are given up to through the just judgment of God.

I might here further reprove the ungodly of this generation for some sins which the Sodomites fell short in, namely the hideous oaths and blasphemies of some profane wretches who hereby belch out their professed enmity against the God of heaven, and offer such open indignity to Him that we may wonder that He is not provoked to rain down fire and brimstone upon them, or to cause the earth to open its mouth to devour them.

This example of Sodom's burning warns the ungodly to repent. Repent, all you ungodly ones, and turn from your evil ways; otherwise your iniquities, like those of the Sodomites, will be your ruin; otherwise God's judgment will overtake you and surprise you, and you shall not be able to bear it; otherwise you shall be destroyed suddenly, and that without remedy. But see in this instance the fruit of ungodliness, the wages of sin, the bitter issue and effect of flesh-pleasing and sensuality. You see that God can be angry, and that His anger burns worse than fire when it is kindled.

If you do not repent, God may bring some dreadful temporal judgments upon you. You have seen much in your days: plague, fire, sword. You have heard of more in former days. You do not know what further calamities may be brought upon this city and nation. God may bring plague and famine together, so that such who do not fall suddenly by the plague shall be consumed more leisurely by famine. He shall bring a famine of bread and a famine of hearing the Word at the same time. And in this the body shall starve and die, and the soul shall starve and be damned and perish everlastingly. God may bring fire and the sword at the same time: your houses may be set on fire and your persons massacred at the same time.

And, alas! What will you who are ungodly do in a time of general calamity? If the pestilence should walk about your streets, if the evil arrows of famine should fly about your ears, if fire should consume your bodies, if the sword should be made drunk with your blood, if death should sit in your window, if all things should be turned into uproar and confusion; then, as for you who drink iniquity like water and load yourselves with guilt daily, you who are profane and ungodly, and spend your time in idleness and all kinds of luxury, sleeping during the harvest and shutting your ears against all the offers of grace and mercy which have been made to you—what will become of you in the winter of affliction? What comfort can you have upon a bed of sickness? What refuge will you have in a time of trouble?

A godly man has his God to fly to in times of greatest danger and distress; and there he shall find entertainment and welcome. But where will you fly? God is your enemy! God will laugh at your calamity (Proverbs 1:26)! Sinners, what will you do in the evil day which may overtake you here on earth, when all refuge and support shall fail you, when your comforts and enjoyments shall be taken from you, when God shall smite you and conscience bite you, when friends forsake you, when the black catalog of your sins shall be spread before you and grim death shall appear unto you, bidding you to come down into the grave; when the devil shall wait for you, to drag you down into hell!

Oh, the confusion that you shall then be in when you perceive that you cannot live, and yet you dare not die; when you feel your eyestrings crack and your heartstrings break, and your souls are now coming forth from their ruinous habitation, where they will become prey to devils, and be immediately conveyed to a place of torments! Think, oh, think what your horror is likely to be here if you are awakened in the evil day through the apprehension of future judgments. What, then, will your horror be if you do not repent when the future and last judgment has come, and Christ has come in flaming fire to take vengeance upon you! He shall rain on you fire and brimstone and a horrible tempest. But of this matter, I will speak more when I come to treat the everlasting burnings of hell, which the Lord Jesus will condemn all the ungodly unto at the last day.

I shall only say that the burnings of hell will not only exceed the burnings of Sodom and Gomorrah in fierceness and duration (as through God's help I shall show in the third part of this discourse), but also the fire of hell will be more intolerable to you than it was to the Sodomites themselves (however vile sinners they were). Matthew 11:24: "But I say unto you that it shall be more tolerable for the land of Sodom in the day of judgment."

As your sins, which have enjoyed the means of grace, are aggravated beyond the sins of Sodom in this respect, so your condemnation will be the greater, and your punishment more sore and intolerable, if you do not now take warnings to repent.

Chapter 9

Application to the Righteous

Lot's escaping out of the overthrow of Sodom and Gomorrah is an example for the encouragement of the righteous. Whatever judgment the Lord brings upon the wicked and ungodly here, you who are righteous shall escape. God will hide you in the day of His anger. When a deluge of judgments shall break in upon the ungodly, God will provide an ark for you; when God rains a horrible tempest of fire and brimstone upon the wicked, He will provide a Zoar for you. God will either keep you from the judgment itself which befalls others, or else He will keep you in it, and from that fiery indignation which is mingled with it. Be sure you shall be kept from the horrible tempest of fire and brimstone which shall beat upon the head of the wicked at last, when the heavens shall be on fire and pass away with a great noise, and the elements shall be on fire and melt with fervent heat; when the earth shall be on fire, and all things here below in flames; when the wrath of the sin-avenging God shall break forth like a deluge upon the ungodly world, and they shall be cast together into the lake which burns with fire and brimstone. Heaven shall be your ark, your Zoar, where you shall be in safety, and made happy in the full enjoyment of God unto all eternity.

Away, then, with fear and dread. Whatever the frowns and threatenings of men are, though floods of the ungodly may surround you, though the wrath of wicked men like fire is kindled against you, yet, being righteous, you are safe. Since God is for you, neither men nor devils shall be permitted to do you any real harm. God is your dwelling place. God is your hiding place. You are under His wing while you remain here, and you shall hereafter lie in His bosom forever.

Fire and Brimstone

Part Two: From Earth in the Burning of Mount Etna

Chapter 1

Introduction

The history of Sodom and Gomorrah's flames and destruction by fire and brimstone from heaven may seem incredible to some who either are ignorant of the power of God (whereby He can do whatsoever He pleases, as appears evidently in the mighty works thereof, which could not be effected without the hand of Omnipotence), and who do not know how fierce and hot His anger is which burns in His breast towards sinners, especially such sinners as the Sodomites were, which would quickly put the whole world into flames did not His infinite patience restrain it for a while from breaking forth in its rage and fury—or who give no credit to the divine authority of the Scriptures (of whom there are too many in our age and nation), which relates this judgment on those wicked cities.

This, however, being indeed the Word of God (as might be proven by many unanswerable arguments), the record of these events is undoubtedly true, and may as firmly be believed as anything may be certainly known which is the object of sense or demonstrable by reason. The future flames of fire and brimstone in hell are discredited by such atheists and antiscripturists, and little believed by most, as appears by their secure walking in the broad way of sin which leads to that place of most dreadful and eternal burning.

Therefore, by way of appendix to Sodom's burning, and by way of introduction to the burning of hell, I shall treat Etna, or Mount Gibel's burning with fire and brimstone out of the bowels of the earth, especially in the eruption of it last year. This was a thing so recent and so near, and attested to by eyewitnesses, it could have been easily disproved had it been false; but it has *not* been disproved. I suppose it will find credit with most, and may be of greater use than has yet been made of, from the relation we have had so barely of the thing without any mention made of the name of God or of His hand, or the end which He may have in such wonderful and stupendous burnings.

It is from the soul that the body has its life and motion, its beauty and luster. When the soul is separated, the body becomes a breathless, lifeless, ghastly carcass, subject to putrefaction. The whole world is full of God, every pile of grass; yea, the meanest thing which is the object of our eye, or any other sense, carries an impression of God; especially the greater works of creation and providence bear large characters of the Deity, and have "praise unto the Lord" written more legibly upon them. Although God is not the soul of the world, as some have affirmed, yet the whole has its beauty from Him, and so far are any works truly admirable and great as God is taken notice of in them.

The sun, moon, and stars, and the whole frame of the heavens, are most great and illustrious as by their brightness and motion they declare the glory of the Lord their Maker and Ruler. The earth and sea, and all things in both, as they set forth God's infinite power and wisdom and goodness, so far are they most worthy of our observation and admiration.

All the good things we receive are only so far truly good to us as we perceive them as handed to us by God; and God's hand in afflictions also sweetens them to us when we are persuaded of the Author's love and design for our good in them. To leave God out, therefore, in the consideration of any work, is to leave out that which is chiefly remarkable. Without Him we see but the carcass without the soul, without life and beauty.

The design, therefore, of this treatise concerning Etna's late burning is to turn our eye upward towards God, so that we take notice of Him and give Him the glory of this work, which is the wonder of all unto whom the notice thereof has come.

There are six things which I shall briefly treat:

1. The mountain of Etna, or Gibel, in general.

2. The antecedents of this mountain's eruption.

3. The eruption of fire and brimstone itself from the mountain.

4. The concomitants of this eruption.

5. The cause of this eruption.

6. The use and application which we should make of it.

Chapter 2

The Mountain of Etna or Gibel in General

Etna is a mountain on the island of Sicily, which is surrounded by the Tyrrhenian Sea, a small distance from Italy, in one part of it, unto which ancient writers think it was joined by an isthmus, or neck of land, unto the mainland of Italy. But by the violent beating of the sea upon that neck it was divided asunder.

The height and size of Etna or Gibel are very great. Some affirm it to be ten miles, others fifteen miles from the head to the foot; the girth to be three or four miles. Toward its head it is rocky and steep, and some part of it is always covered with snow. Towards the middle of it, it is beautified with trees and woods; towards the bottom it is enriched with corn and vines, and is exceedingly fruitful. The hill has two shoulders eastward and between them is an eminent head in the middle which may be seen at a distance of fifty leagues (as some affirm) by sailors on the sea. But that which has rendered this mountain most famous has not been so much the size of it as it has been the smoking head and flaming mouth thereof, of which both ancient and modern authors have written.

Diogenes Laertius makes mention of Mount Etna. He says that Empedocles, the philosopher, was famous for having thrown himself into its flaming mouth so that, not being found by his companions, they might think he was translated to heaven and made an immortal god. But the fire of the hill cast forth one of his brazen sandals and the deceit was discovered. And so, instead of purchasing for himself the reputation of a god, he revealed himself, in that respect, to be beneath a man.

Horace also recorded the same:

> Empedocles, himself into the mouth doth throw
> Of burning Etna, that not being found below
> He might be famed a god immortal.

In his second book of natural history, Pliny writes of this hill: "Among the miracles of mountains, Etna flames always by night, and affords matter for perpetual fire."

Justin, in his fourth *Book of History,* gives the reason why the burning of Mount Etna has lasted for so many ages.

In his sixth book of geography, Strabo tells us of Etna's open mouth, whereby it breathes forth flames and casts forth fiery stones.

Ovid said, concerning Etna, "It vomits fire out of its fierce mouth." Seneca describes Etna in his *Thestes,* "Resounding with eternal tunnels, or breathing holes of fire."

But Virgil gave the most notable description of Etna's burning in his third *Book of Aeneas:*

> Through horrid falls within, like noise of thunder,
> Mount Etna sounds as if 'twould break asunder.
> Thence first a cloud breaks forth as black as night,
> With pitchy curls, with sparks like stars to flight.

Then follow globes of flames, which mount aloft,
As if to kiss the orbs of heaven they sought.
The bottom fire like boiling furnace glows,
Which melts the hardest stones and upward throws
Great rocks through th'air with groans.
The same doth go,
That great Enceladus do lie below
Who, being thunderstruck, and on him thrown
Huge Etna Mount, with weight to keep him down;
When weary he shifts sides and turns about
He shakes the Mount, his breath in flames goes out.
As a furnace mouth, the heavens above
Are clothed with smoke. Trinacria trembles.

I shall add but one more author, and that is a late geographer named Verenius, who in his first book of geography both describes this mount and gives relations of a notable eruption of fire not much more than a hundred years ago:

Etna in Sicily, now called Mount Gibel, is most famous, from whose top the flames and smoke may be seen at a very great distance on the Mediterranean Sea; and although the casting forth of fire and smoke is continual, yet sometimes it breathes forth with more force and fury. In the year 1537, from the first day of May until the 12th, the whole island of Sicily trembled, and then was heard a great roaring and cracking noise, as if great pieces of ordnance had been discharged. After this followed the ruin and overthrow of many buildings throughout the whole island. This raging continued for eleven whole days together, in which time the earth (on the side of the mount) was rent, and opened itself in wide clefts; from whence issued forth flames of fire with such force and strength that all things within 15 miles of Etna were thereby consumed and burnt up. A little after, the cup which is on the top of the mount, for three whole days together, cast forth such a large quantity of burning coals and ashes that they were dispersed not only throughout the whole island, but they were also carried over the sea into Italy. Yea, some ships two hundred leagues from Sicily received damage hereby in their voyage to Venice.

There have been other great eruptions of fire from this mountain besides what is the usual, which writers have recorded, but none that I ever read of like this last one, the account of which follows.

Chapter 3

The Antecedents of the Late Eruption
of Mount Etna

I t was on Friday night, March 8, 1668, that a great noise and roaring was heard from the bowels and mouth of Mount Etna, which sounded far and near, more loud and dreadful than that of great guns in the camps or in the ships of enemies. The roaring of the sea in a storm, when it lifts up its waves on high and dashes them with violence upon the great rocks and lofty shores, was nothing by comparison. And it may be questioned whether the loud cracks of thunder, when with the greatest fierceness they break through the thickest cloud, ever sounded so terrible (although this has sometimes caused great men, full of guilt, to run under their beds for fear), as this roaring and bellowing of Mount Etna did that night; which, being in the silent night, when all things were hushed and other noises asleep, was heard with the greater plainness and astonishment.

This awakened the inhabitants of Catania, a city fifteen miles distant from the mount, especially those who lived upon the borders and sides thereof; whereby they were surprised with great fear, possibly much as the wicked world shall be when they shall hear the sound of the last trumpet, summoning them to judgment.

The roaring of the mountain was accompanied at the same time with a shaking and trembling of the earth, which must have added to the trembling and horror of the people who dwelled thereabouts. The city of Catania itself felt the earthquake, and the houses whereof shook so and danced as if they would immediately have tumbled from their foundations. But the earthquake was most violent in the countries and villages nearer unto and upon the sides of the mountain, where there was such a shaking and concussion that people could not stand on their legs without holding onto one another, but reeled and staggered to and fro, as if they had been overcome by drink. The houses of many were so cleft and torn that, first, shaking out their inhabitants, who with all speed hastened out of them, they quickly tumbled to the ground. The whole town of Nicolesi was utterly ruined by the earthquake; the towns of Padara and Trecastager were, the greatest part of them, ruined and destroyed.

The sight of such ruins before the eye, feeling such motions and shakings underfoot, and the sound of such roarings from the mountain in the ear surely struck those people with more terror and amazement than was upon the inhabitants of London when their houses were in flames before them and they were forced to seek lodging in the fields.

Besides this, the fear of those perplexed people was increased when they saw the ground cleaving in several places around them, and the earth opening its mouth, as if it would have devoured them, as formerly the rebellious Korah, Dathan, and Abiram were swallowed up. This put them upon the wing to fly with all haste from those parts, who in great amazement, with hair standing on end, joints trembling, and distracted looks, hardly able to speak, brought the tidings of these things to the city of Catania.

Chapter 4

The Eruption Itself of Fire and Brimstone
from Mount Etna

After warning was given by the voice of the mountain and the shaking of the earth to fly from that place of danger and threatened ruin, on Monday, March 11, there were three great eruptions on the side of the mountain, besides the smoke and flames which issued forth from the mouth at the top thereof. The breaches and clefts of the earth were a half mile in compass, out of which a horrible, burning flood came forth and, more fiercely than any floods of water could do, ran down the sides of the mount. It was the fire contained before within the bowels of the mountain, too big and great to vent itself at the top, that forced its way through the sides and made doors for itself, breaking forth with such noise and rage as was terrible to hear and behold.

This fire, in its first vent, folding itself in great flames as if more than a thousand houses had been burning together, mounted up towards heaven no less than a hundred yards in height. This was accompanied by such a roaring noise, far beyond what was heard before at the mouth of the hill, as if more than a thousand cannons had been discharged at once; there vast stones were shot forth, some of them three hundred pounds in weight, which were

mounted aloft very high in the air, and with great
force were thrown many miles from the place. This
grew into a furious tempest, not of rain or hail, but
something far more dreadful, of burning coals and
ashes and suffocating smoke, which beat down
upon the country all around, something like that
rain of fire and brimstone which fell upon Sodom.

But that which was most notable in these eruptions was the stream and flood of fire which in liquid melted matter gushed forth at the breaches. We
read in Isaiah 30:33 of a stream of brimstone kindled
by the breath of God which runs in burning Tophet.
Such was the stream of fire and brimstone which
came forth from this burning mountain. The flames
of it were blue, like burning brimstone; the color
was fiery red, like melted brass; the motion of it was
like quicksilver. This stream, wherein great stones
the size of an ordinary table were seen to swim, came
forth at the sides of the mountain, running down
like a mighty torrent, and, meeting with a hill, divided itself into two currents. These spread themselves; one of them was in some places at least six
miles wide, and was judged to be fifteen yards deep.
In its progress, this stream ran in upon a lake of
four fathoms of water, four miles in compass, which
it both filled up and raised a hill of ragged stones
and rocks upon it. The composition of this fiery
stream was judged to be sulphur, nitrogen, lead,
iron, brass, and other metals, melted with the
vehement heat of the fire.

We have read of a deluge and flood of waters
which drowned the old world, and other lesser in-
undations which have drowned particular places;

but I do not know of any history which tells of a deluge and flood of fire such as this, which devoured and destroyed whatever lay in its way. The late relating of the eruption of Mount Etna tells us that wherever it passed, it left large heaps of its congealed matter with which it covered and burned the earth, melting the walls of castles and houses, throwing down all before it. Nothing could be found that was able to resist its force or quench its burning. Water rather added to its fury. Wherever it passed, it left dreadful marks behind it, leveling some hills and raising others, so much changing the situation that not the least trace of any place or town which was in its way remained. Nothing was to be seen but confused heaps of ragged stones which yielded a noisome terror and astonishment in all who beheld it.

The first breaking forth of this burning flood of fire was on Monday, March 11. It divided itself into several lesser streams, and filled the whole country thereabouts with fire and brimstone. In many places where these streams came, great flames were seen to arise together, with thick smoke as from the mouths of so many great furnaces.

After the flood of fire had come down the mountain and towards the base, which is not so steep, it did not move with that swiftness as before; yet nothing could divert its course, but it overturned and consumed all wherever it came. The first streams continued their course for twelve days; and after hopes that the fury of the fire had spent itself, on Friday, March 22, the mountain roared and thundered, smoked and flamed again most hideously at the mouth; it shook and trembled throughout most dreadfully to the very foundations; it cast forth such heaps of cinders, stones, and ragged rocks out of its bosom and bowels that they grew together and were raised into two large and high hills. And this was accompanied with another stream of its liquid, melted matter, which overtook the former currents and thrust them forward with great fury.

But on March 25, the mountain bellowed with a greater noise than ever before, and was shaken with such violence and force that a large part of the head and top fell into the breast and bowels at a depth of half a mile, as some judge. Then it issued forth fiery streams in such great abundance that, joining forces with the former, they made great havoc and desolation, destroying the habitations of no less than 27,000 persons. The towns of La Guardia, Malpassa, Campo Rotundo, La Potielli, Antonino, Pietro, Mosterbianco, Monpileri, Falicchi, and Placchi were wholly consumed and ruined. Yea, the image of the Blessed Lady of the Annunciation (so highly reverenced by the superstitious papists, unto which many resorted in pilgrimage from remote parts) was not spared. Whatever power the intercession of that virgin lady has with her Son in heaven for persons here on earth (as the papists ridiculously fancy), yet nothing could now avail to secure her image from being swallowed up by this devouring fiery stream. From this all may see that there was no difference between the stones of that image and those of the other buildings in that place which equally felt the force of the fire.

Other places were ruined in part, such as

Mascalucia, Giovanni de Galermo, and many others; and at length the burning streams approached the gates and walls of the city of Catania, in their course destroying fields, gardens, orchards, and vineyards. This filled the inhabitants with such fear that, for the greatest part, they removed themselves and their goods out of the city. Yet, whatever the danger and fear was, the Lord preserved the city from being swallowed up by these devouring streams. Part of these streams were congealed on the land; one of them emptied itself under the walls of the castle into the sea in four fathoms of water, which held its current in the sea two fathoms high above it, and, to the astonishment of all spectators, burned in the sea itself for a great while. Making its way into the sea a mile long and a mile wide, it was not quenched by the water of the sea until, having spent itself, it did, of itself, congeal.

Chapter 5

*The Concomitants of the Eruption
and Burning of Mount Etna*

While the mountains of Etna vomited flames of fire at the top, and streams of fire at the sides, accompanied with such dreadful tremblings and shakings of the earth, other things were also observed at the same time. One of these was the swelling of the sea to a great and unaccustomed height, with great raging and roaring waves. The floods of waters seemed to lift up their heads to see this dreadful spectacle of the floods of fire; and the waves of the sea lifted their voice in great tumult, being amazed at the horrid aspect of the waves and streams of fire and brimstone.

The clouds were gathered thickly in the sky, and arrayed the heavens with black attire, hiding the comfortable and refreshing beams of the sun from the light which sometimes peeped through the clouds. It was with a pale countenance, as if it had been struck with fear, and dared not appear in such a dismal place.

Storms of rain often powered down from the clouds, which seemed to weep in compassion, to weep floods of tears, endeavoring thereby to contribute some help to extinguish the flames; but all the rain which fell was so far from quenching or allaying it that it only the more increased and exasperated the fury of the fire which hereby burned so much more fiercely.

In the city there was a danger of the houses being overthrown by the winds and the earthquake, or of their being devoured and swallowed up by the deluge of fire. In the fields and countries there was a danger of being destroyed by thieves and robbers who took advantage of the people's confusion to set upon them, murdering many, and robbing them of their choicest things which they had saved from their ruined houses.

Great was the dread and terror which now possessed the hearts of the people. Our Savior therefore tells us in Luke 21:25–26 that "on earth there should be distress of nations with perplexity, the sea and the waves roaring, and men's hearts failing them for fear, and for looking after those things which are coming upon the earth." Such was the distress and perplexity of these people. It is said that people ran with cries and lamentations about the city and country, expecting nothing but to be swallowed up or consumed by the fire, having no other apprehensions but of death and a general conflagration.

Had the Christian religion taken place there in the purity and power thereof, it might have upheld the spirits of the sincere and established Christians against overwhelming fear and amazement in all those storms and danger. If it may be said of the virtuous man, much more may it be said of the truly religious: "Though the frame of the earth and world should crack and be dissolved, yet such a one would be undaunted under its ruins." Such, when the

moutain was dissolved and melted with fervent heat
into floods of burning fire, might look upon death
(that utmost the fire could bring upon them) with
an unappalled countenance; yea, with great confidence and comfort because of their well-grounded
hopes of rest and happiness in heaven, whose habitations prepared for them there are beyond the
reach of any earthly fire to consume.

But no wonder if the blind, superstitious papists,
whose worship is mingled with such vanity and
idolatry, are filled with such dread and horror, especially the more notorious sinners among them.
Surely the consciences of most of them are now
awakened; the stings and lashes whereof, no doubt,
above all other things at this time increased their
terror.

But what course did they take to divert God's
anger, which so visibly broke forth in these flames
and fire from the burning mountain, and for the
prevention of the threatened ruin? They did not
take themselves to their knees, to fasting and prayer
in any way of God's prescribing; they did not apply
themselves by faith unto the blood of Christ to appease the wrath of the angry God. No, it is related
that the religious appeared everywhere with much
devotion, carrying in procession their relics, especially those of St. Agatha, the famous martyr of
Catania, in which they reposed no small confidence.
This was followed by a great multitude of people,
mortifying themselves with whips and other signs of
penance. And the bishop of the place, followed by
the clergy and an infinite number of people, went
into solemn processions out of the city of Catania

unto Monte de St. Sophia, carrying out with greatest devotion their choicest relics, and, upon an altar, erected in view of the mountain, exposed them, whereby they celebrated Mass, and used exorcisms accustomed upon such extraordinary occasions.

This is how blindly and sottishly superstitious these people are. But is the anger of the Lord hereby appeased? No, it is so much the more increased; and they cannot charm the noise and flames of the mountain with all their exorcisms. But all this while they continue in their superstitious exercises. I read that the mountain ceased not as before with excessive roaring to throw up its smoke and flames with extraordinary violence, and an abundance of great stones were carried through the air, some of them falling within their view, though at ten miles' distance from the eruption. This was an open rebuke of them for their superstition, which was so odious and abominable in the sight of God.

Chapter 6

The Cause of the Eruption of Mount Etna

The supreme cause of the flames and fiery streams which broke forth from the bowels of Mount Etna was the Lord, who is not only the Being of beings, but also the Cause of causes. No matter what was the second cause, God was the first cause of all the works of nature in the world, being effected by Him who is the God of nature, and by Him everything has its being, as well as its virtue and operation. Job 9:10: "He doth great things past finding out, yea, and wonders without number." Among the wonderful works of God, this is none of the least.

In miracles, God works more immediately; and in wonders, God works more remarkably than in ordinary works. Moreover, this eruption of fire, which made such a dreadful devastation of houses, carried with it the plain face of a judgment; and every judgment is from God as the Judge of the world. God is in no way the Author of sin, but He is the Author of all penal evil; the anger of the Lord not only smoked, but broke forth into a flame; it was the breath of the Lord that kindled this stream, which overturned and swallowed up so many habitations.

And surely the inhabitants of the place had been blowing on the coals of God's anger before this by their sins. It was not without cause from themselves that this judgment was brought upon them. The distance of this place from Rome is but little, and the difference between them in idolatry and all sorts of wickedness is reported to be less. Sicily has drunk deep of the cup of fornication, which is in the hand of the Romish whore, and God made some of them drink something of the cup of His wrath and indignation. Sodomy itself is of frequent practice in those parts, and God brings ruin like unto that of Sodom upon their houses by streams of fire and brimstone, though through infinite patience their persons were preserved.

When this fire was first kindled is not known, the burning of the mountain being more ancient than any history can remember. What the poets feign concerning the war of the giants with the gods, and their casting down of great Enceladus with thunder and keeping him down with vast mountains, and this of Etna being thrown upon his head—that this fire was kindled by his hot breath is as ridiculous as it is fabulous.

Some are of the opinion that there are fountains of fire underground as well as of water, and that in the bosom and bowels of the earth God has laid up treasures of this element, enclosing it in vast caverns as in so many storehouses. This subterranean fire they assign as the cause of hot baths, and that Mount Etna, as also Vesuvius, with other flaming mountains, which geographers and travelers tell us are to be seen in all parts of the world, are the breathing holes of this fire. But Scripture is wholly silent about any such work of God

there. We read of the earth, of the gathering
together of the waters, and of the fountains of the
great deep, but we read nothing of any fountains of
fire mingled with either of these elements. And the
laying up of this element in store, in a place so low,
when naturally it tends upwards, is not easy to
conceive. Besides, who has ever descended into the
depths of the earth to search and find out these
depths of fire?

Justin gives other reasons for this fire: "The earth
in that place being so thin and hollow and
penetrable by the winds, and the soil being so
sulphurous, and so fit matter for begetting and
nourishing fire, the motion of the wind closed in
and kindled the fire which belched forth in smoke
and flames. And hence it is that the burning of Etna
has endured for so many ages." Unto this he adds,
speaking of the fall of the waters: "The cause of
Etna's perpetual fire is from the great and perpetual
fill of the water near at hand which carries down the
wind and air, and suffocates it at the bottom;
whence it breathes away through some crevices of
the earth towards the mountain, and this kindles
and blows the flames."

Another man assigns the cause more clearly:
"Mount Etna has caverns and vaults full of sulphur,
which reach so far as the sea, which vaults, receiving
into them the waves of the sea, wind is begotten
thereby; which wind, being violently moved, begets
the fire out of the sulphur." And therefore he tells us
that as the east and south winds blow, so this
mountain more or less vomits up sparks and fire.

Lucretius sets forth the cause in this manner:

The mountain of Etna hollow is throughout,
With stones of flint its caves are lined about,
Whereby it is held up; the wind is there
In every cave begot by moved air.
Through motion heats engendered in the earth,
Thence fire springs forth and flames have birth.
Besides, against the mountain's roots, the main
Break her swollen waves and swallow them again,
From whence unto the top of its ascent
The undermining caves have their extent,
Through which the billows breathe and
      cast forth flames
With showers of stone ashes.

Chapter 7

The Use of the Burning of Mount Etna

These late dreadful eruptions of fire and brimstone from Mount Etna should carry our eyes upward unto God, the Author thereof. The Lord has been lately upon the earth. He has shown Himself in great majesty. A fire has devoured before Him, and it has been very tempestuous round about. A smoke has gone out of His mouth and coals have been under His feet. He has clothed Himself with flames, and has of late appeared very terribly in these European parts. He has not only kindled fires in houses and cities, turning them into ashes and ruinous heaps, but He has also kindled a fire in a great mountain, which has broken forth with a great flame.

Psalm 29:3–8: "The voice of the Lord is powerful, and full of majesty; the voice of the Lord is upon the waters, the God of glory thundereth; the voice of the Lord is upon many waters; the voice of the Lord shaketh the wilderness, and maketh Lebanon and Sirion like a young unicorn." Surely majesty and power have been in God's voice, which was heard from this mountain. The voice of the Lord has sounded from the earth; the God of glory has thundered out of the bowels of a great mountain whereby the foundations thereof have been so shaken, as if he would have overturned it in His anger. Formerly the Lord brought forth streams of water out of the hard rock; and lately He has brought forth streams of fire out of the deep earth. This is the Lord's doing, and should it be marvelous in our eyes? If we wonder at the work, let us wonder more at the Worker; if we admire to hear of such floods of fire, we have more reason to admire God's infinite power, which has effected this.

The relating of Etna's burning should awaken impenitent sinners out of their carnal security. Let them consider the hand of God herein, and that the same God who kindled such a fire in the mountain is highly incensed against them, so long as they allow and indulge themselves in any sinful practices; and that the fire of God's anger, which is kindled in His breast against them, is ten thousand times more dreadful than the fire which was kindled in the bowels of the mountain. Let them consider that God is preparing the fire of hell for them, which shall burn everlastingly, if they do not repent. The same God who has the power to kindle a fire in the earth has power to kindle the fires of hell; and He who has power to keep the fires of this mountain alive for thousands of years has the power to keep the fire of hell alive for eternity. This He can do, and this He will do. And, oh, how fearful a thing will it be to be thrown into everlasting flames (of which more largely in the next discourse)!

Awake, then, all you sons and daughters of sleep and security! Awake, you children of the night and darkness, and all you workers of iniquity!

Look up and see how powerful and terrible the Lord is, and how unable you are to make resistance once His hand shall take hold of you with vengeance. God's anger now only smokes against you; ere long it will break into a flame which will burn to the lowest hell and shall never be extinguished.

Let me, therefore, persuade you to break off your sins by repentance, and apply yourselves to Christ by faith so that the anger of the Lord towards you may be appeased, and that, being reconciled, you may escape the dreadful effects of His displeasure.

Chapter 8

The Burning of London That May Be

The relating of Etna's burning should lead us to the consideration of the burnings which *may* be and the burnings which *shall* be. First, consider the burnings which *may* be.

Our dear and beloved city of London may be burned again with fire—not only the suburbs and Southwark, and the remaining timber houses which the last fire spared, but also the newly built houses of brick. Many of them, it has been proven, can burn; for no building on earth is a sufficient defense against fire. I don't think we are in danger of any such fire as that of Etna, to break forth under our feet from out of the bowels of the earth, but we may be in danger of a fire forged in hell. I mean, some devilish, wicked men may be contriving the burning of the city. It is not long ago that our flourishing city was laid waste by devouring flames.

The depositions given before the magistrates concerning the hands of the papists set on work herein are not forgotten; the principles of the papists, which will allow them to murder princes, blow up parliaments, massacre people, and burn cities, if those people are "heretics," as they call them, have not been altered. The attempts of late to set houses in this city on fire have been made evident; and I wish that there were no cursed design now on foot among such vile persons to burn our city and massacre our people. It is not amiss for us to think of what may be. There may be houses falling down upon our heads in the street, and we may be crushed thereby to pieces, as some have been. This should put us in continual preparation for death, and much more so when we are in danger of death in many other ways. If you should hear a cry at midnight, "The papists have come!"; that fireballs are flying about the streets, that fires are kindled in several parts of the city at the same time, and that bloody cutthroats stand ready to butcher naked people as they come forth from burning houses with their goods; if you should hear the groans and shrieks of your neighbors while they are cruelly massacred by the hands of merciless villains; if, when they approach your doors, you see no way of escaping, but death is inevitable; if you should then be found unprepared for death, when you have no time to prepare, how surprised you would be! How frightened you would be!

It is good to provide for the worst, so that whenever death appears, in whatever shape, it may not prove to be a king of terrors. How happy are those who have made their peace with God, when some men will not be at peace with them. How little reason have those to fear the wrath of any here who are delivered from the wrath to come. How safe is that treasure which is laid up in heaven, far beyond the reach of thief or rust or flames of fire! Get clear evidence of these things. If you are delivered out of the snare of the devil, you need not be afraid of the snares of men. If you are not in danger of hell, you need not be afraid of death; if you have well-grounded hopes of escaping everlasting flames, and of obtaining everlasting joys through your interest in Christ and His purchase, you may smile at the flames on your houses, and laugh at destruction when it comes.

But I hope (if there is such a design, which I neither do nor can affirm) that the Lord will prevent the effusion of our blood and the destruction of our city, which too many may desire. And I hope that if ever they should attempt such a massacre as took place in Paris or Ireland, and seek to mingle our blood and fire together, the Lord will so spirit all true Protestants and Englishmen to stand up so in their own defense, which the law of God and nature will allow, so as by them to bring that destruction upon themselves which they may endeavor, against all law and justice, to bring upon God's people.

Second, Etna's burning should lead us to the consideration of the burnings which *will* be. There are three great burnings that certainly will be:

1. The burning of Rome;
2. The burning of the world;
3. The burning of hell.

Chapter 9

The Burning of Rome

We may be put in mind hereby of the burning of Rome, which certainly will be, of which this eruption of Etna so near to us may be a prognostication and forerunner. That Rome is the Babylon threatened with destruction and fire will be evident if you look into the description given in Revelation 17:1–6:

> And there came one of the seven angels which had the seven vials, and talked with me saying unto me, "Come hither; I will show unto thee the judgment of the great whore that sitteth upon many waters, with whom the kings of the earth have committed fornication, and the inhabitants have been made drunk with the wine of her fornication." So he carried me away in the Spirit into the wilderness. And I saw a woman sit upon a scarlet-colored beast, full of names of blasphemy, having seven heads and ten horns. And the woman was arrayed in purple and scarlet color, and decked with gold and precious stones, and pearls, having a golden cup in her hand, full of abomination and filthiness of her fornication. And upon her forehead was a name written: "Mystery, Babylon the Great, the mother of harlots and abominations of the earth." And I saw the woman drunken with the blood of the saints, and with the blood of the martyrs of Jesus.

That this description is applicable to the papacy of Rome and to no other is evident from every part thereof, as it is explained by the angel in this same chapter, and fulfilled as to every particular in the popedom. We are not to understand it of one particular pope, but of the whole race and succession of them who are called "the great whore, sitting upon many waters, with whom the kings of the earth have committed fornication." This signifies the spiritual fornication committed by them with her, or the idolatry which she drew them to the practice of.

The waters are the people whom she has under subjection; the scarlet-colored beast she sits upon, having seven heads and ten horns, is the great city of Rome and the state thereof; the seven heads signifiy seven mountains upon which Rome was built, therefore she is called "seven-hilled Rome." Moreover, the city is described to be the city which then reigned over the kings of the earth, which was the city of Rome, the imperial seat at that time. The ten horns signify the kings of the earth who give their power to the pope for his support. This whore is called "Babylon, the great mother of harlots, who maketh the nations drunk with the wine of her fornication, and who herself is drunk with the blood of saints and martyrs." And to whom can this be applied but the pope, who intoxicates so many nations as with wine or potions, from whence it comes to pass that they wallow in the filthiness of spiritual fornication, and who has shed so much of the blood of saints for the testimony of Jesus against the Romish superstition and idolatry.

I would digress too far to apply all the parts of

this description with other descriptions in Revelation, and of antichrist in Thessalonians, to the pope of Rome, as I might do, and prove by unanswerable arguments that the pope is the antichrist and Rome spiritual Babylon. That which here we chiefly should mind is the judgment of this great whore. Verse 16: "The ten horns which thou sawest upon the beast shall hate the whore, and shall make her desolate and naked, and shall eat her flesh and burn her with fire."

And throughout chapter 18 we have the destruction and burning of Babylon, or Rome, set forth at length. Verse 2: "Babylon the great is fallen." Verse 4: "Come out of her, My people, that ye partake not of her plagues." Verse 7: "As she hath glorified herself and lived deliciously, so much torment and sorrow give her." Verse 8: "Her plagues shall come in one day, and she shall be utterly burned with fire, for strong is the Lord God who judgeth her." The kings of the earth who committed fornications with her; and merchants and shipmasters shall bewail her when they see the smoke of her burning (verses 9, 11), but in heaven there shall be joy. The Lord will rejoice; the prophets and apostles will rejoice; and all the saints will rejoice in the vengeance which shall then be taken upon her (verse 20).

Rome was standing, and rejoiced when London was burning. And I hope London will be standing, and will much more rejoice when Rome is burning. London was burned but in part; Rome shall be utterly burned with fire. After its fire, London was rebuilt in a great measure; but Rome shall never be rebuilt after this burning. This Babylon, when it falls, shall never rise again. Verse 21: "And a mighty angel took up a stone like a great millstone, and cast it into the sea, saying, 'Thus with violence shall that great city Babylon be thrown down, and shall be found no more at all.' " As a great millstone thrown into the midst of the sea is overwhelmed with water, so shall Rome be overwhelmed with fire. And as a millstone cannot be raised and drawn out of the sea, so Rome, when burned, shall never be raised again out of its ashes and ruins.

Dreadful will be the destruction of Rome when the time of her burning comes. Those who stand afar off for fear of her torments, who have been friends to her, shall lament. What lamentations, then, will there be by such as shall be found in the place itself, when it shall be set on fire around their ears? When the pope and cardinals, and the other inhabitants of that filthy and abominably wicked city, shall be consumed together (as is likely) in the midst of the flames? Oh, the hideous outcries which will then be made in every street, when they are surrounded with fire on all sides, and there is no way left for them to escape; when their houses and wealth and persons shall be consumed by the devouring flames; when God, by such a dreadful fire on earth, shall convey them down to the more dreadful fire of hell!

Then the Lord will avenge all the blood of His saints which, under the anti-Christian tyranny, has been shed for so many generations. Then He will avenge all the idolatry, pride, covetousness, oppression, blasphemy, filthiness, cruelty, and wickedness of Rome. When the grapes of this vine are fully ripe, the angel, with his sharp sickle, will cut it and throw it into the winepress of God's wrath, where it shall be squeezed and crushed to pieces. When their iniquities are full, then their ruin shall come.

And surely the time is not far off. I am much of the persuasion that this generation shall not pass away before God will accomplish what He has threatened concerning Rome's burning and destruction. The last sands of the hour of God's patience seem to be running; the forty-two months seem to be expiring; and the two witnesses who were cruelly slain, it may be, are arising. And then Rome will quickly be falling.

Chapter 10

The Burning of the World

B y the burning of Mount Etna, we may be put in mind also of the burning of the world. I mean, the last general conflagration of the world at its end. Whether Etna's burning is a prognostication of Rome's burning is not so certain; but that it is a prognostication of the world's burning and dissolution by fire may be proven from Scripture. In Luke 21:10–11, our Savior foretold for His disciples what the signs would be of His coming and the end of the world: wars, pestilences, and earthquakes. These suggest fearful sights, and I truly think there has not been a more fearful sight since the days of our Savior than this of the eruption of fire and brimstone from this flaming mountain. The inhabitants of the place expected a general conflagration on them, but we may well say that this fearful sight is a forerunner of the one foretold by Christ, and therefore this should put us in mind of it.

The notice of this great and universal burning of the world we do not get from reason, but from Scripture. The clearest and fullest place to prove it is found in 2 Peter 3:5–7: "By the Word of God the heavens were of old, and the earth standing out of the water and in the water, whereby the world that then was being overflowed with water perished. But the heavens and earth which are now, by the same Word, kept in store, reserved unto fire against the day of judgment, and perdition of ungodly men." And verse 10: "The day of the Lord will come as a thief in the night, in which the heavens shall pass away with a great noise, and the elements shall melt with fervent heat; the earth also and the works that are therein shall be burned up." Here note:

First, as the world of old was drowned by water, so the world that now is shall be consumed by fire. As certainly as the former was, so certainly shall the latter be; and as dreadful as the flood was to sinners on that day, so dreadful, and much more dreadful, will the fire be to sinners on the last day.

Second, it is by the word of the Lord that the general conflagration shall be effected. By the word of the Lord the world was made, by the word of the Lord the world was drowned, and by the word of the Lord the world shall be burned. In His Word He has foretold it, and by His word He will effect it.

Third, the heavens and earth are said to be reserved in store for fire. When the old world was drowned, it was only the earth and the inhabitants thereof; the heavens were untouched. The earth remained intact, and the same earth appeared afterwards when the flood was drawn off by God. But at the last day the heavens and earth too shall be dissolved by fire; not by subterranean fire, as some imagine, as if when the world was drowned the fountains of the great deep were opened and the waters which before were kept in storehouses were brought forth and overwhelmed the earth. Similarly they imagine that there are fountains of fire in the bowels of the earth, and that fire is kept in store-houses, all which shall then be opened and the fire shall break forth in a more dreadful flame than ever was seen at Mount Etna, setting the whole fabric of the world on fire.

As I said before, nothing of this is found in Scripture. It is said that the heavens and earth are kept in store for fire; but it is not said that fire is kept in store for them. Besides, how can we conceive that any subterranean fire could have the power to reach and dissolve the heavens?

Fourth, the time of this burning of the world shall be at the day of judgment and perdition of the ungodly, called in verse 10 "the day of the Lord." It will be at the day of Christ's appearance to judgment, when He shall be revealed from heaven with His mighty angels in flaming fire to take vengeance on the ungodly world. He will have already raised up the righteous from the dead, and will have gathered them together from the four winds, and called them up into the clouds, and openly acknowledged and acquitted them and set them in a place of safety. For as Noah and his family were hidden from the deluge of water in the ark, so the Lord will hide all the righteous under His wing from the fire. Then, having examined and sentenced the wicked unto eternal perdition, it will most likely be the time for Him to set the world on fire. And all the wicked of all generations will remain in the midst of those flames until the whole is consumed, except for those who will then be cast into a place of more dreadful burning, I mean, the everlasting fire of hell.

The time cannot be far off; the Lord will come

very shortly. Hebrews 10:37: "Yet a little while and He that shall come will come, and will not tarry." And the Lord will come suddenly, "as a thief in the night." When the world is secure, and no more expects it than the old world did the flood or the Sodomites the fire, then the Lord will come.

Fifth, here is a more particular description of the burning of the world. Verse 10: "The heavens shall pass away with a great noise, and the elements shall melt with fervent heat; the earth also and the works that are therein shall be burned up." And then verse 11: "All these things shall be dissolved." The heavens shall be in flames, and the frame of them will crack with a hideous noise, far beyond whatever before sounded in the ear of any mortal. Like a great scroll they shall be rolled together and fly away out of sight. All the elements also shall feel the force of this fire, and hereby be melted and consumed into nothing. The elementary fire, air and water shall all melt and evaporate with this fervent heat, so as to be no more; but especially the earth and works thereof shall be the subject of these burnings. All the buildings, all the houses and towns and cities of the world shall be on fire together; all the great and vast mountains shall be in flames. Yea, the great woods, plains, and fields, the whole earth, from the very bottom of its foundations, shall be on fire and shall be burned up.

Oh, what a dreadful fire will this be! It will be dreadful to behold it; how much more dreadful will it be to feel it! To be in the midst of it! The wicked shall be passing to the eternal flames of hell when they will see the heavens on fire, the air on fire, the water on fire, the earth on fire, the cities on fire, the fields on fire, and themselves on fire—head, back, breast, belly, hands, arms, legs, feet, every part on fire. And this fire is such a one that torments them, but is not able to consume them. When they see the heavens which have endured so long melt, stones broken, and the hardest metals dissolved by the fervent heat of this fire, and yet their bodies made so strong that their flesh shall not be consumed hereby, oh, how fearful will this be! Tongue cannot utter, thought cannot conceive the anguish of the wicked on this day, and in this place of fire.

Thomas Doolittle, in his book *Rebuke for Sin after God's Burning Anger,* passionately sets forth the woe of the ungodly through this fire:

> Shall all this world be dissolved, and all the works thereof burned up with fire? Then fear and tremble, all you who are ungodly, and yet in your sins; for, behold, the Lord will kindle a fire in His anger, and the wrath of the Lord shall blow it up till it increases into such flames as your eyes never yet beheld, which shall burn unto the lowest hell; which shall consume the earth with her increase, and set on fire the foundations of the mountains. Then God will heap up mischiefs upon your heads, and rain down fires and a horrible tempest upon your souls. Then He will spend His arrows upon you; then shall you be scorched with devouring heat, and be destroyed with bitter destruction.
>
> Oh, what will you do? Where will you go? To whom will you speak to plead for you with the Lord? Just imagine the dreadfulness of your case, the horror that your hearts shall then be filled with, by supposing that you were shut up

in some place, some great and large dwelling that is filled with pitch, oil, brimstone, and all such things that are fit fuel for greedy flames. Imagine the fire kindled, and every part of the house as hot as a fiery furnace, and the pitch and brimstone dropping down upon your heads, and you could neither get out of it nor die in it. Instead you must live to feel the burning heat of such kindled, raging flames. You cry out for help, but no one can succor you; you call for someone to rescue you, but no one can, nor dares come near you. If you go from one room to another, you find no place nor corner that is not kindled; if you go to the top, the fire is there; if you go to the bottom, the fire is there.

The bars of the windows are bars of iron, the doors of brass, so that if you attempt to break the one or open the other, you only burn your fingers when you lay hold of the bars or doors, that have been made fiery by the flames. The walls are all of brick and stone, so that there is no breaking through, but they are like an oven that is filled with an even greater heat. Suppose that this fire should last a week; and, were it possible for you to live so long therein, how miserable would you look upon yourselves to be? How sad, how wretched, how deplorable would your condition be?

Why, beyond, beyond, infinitely beyond this will be the case of the ungodly at the dissolution of the world. No heart can now conceive, no tongue can now express what shall be the misery and the woe of sinners at that day, before they go to be tormented in the flames of hell. There shall be fire above them, fire beneath them, fire within them, fire round about them; the heavens shall melt and scald their heads; the earth shall burn and scorch their feet. If they run into their houses, they are all flames; if they hasten into the fields and woods, the trees and grass are all burning; if they dig into the earth, flames of fire are flashing in their faces every time they open it; if they go into the dens and caverns of the earth, behold, they are all fiery red, many times hotter than the fiery furnace; if they would hide themselves under the rocks and mountains, behold, they are removed and passed away. There is no shelter or shade where they might sit and rest and cool themselves.

Oh, the horrible outcries! the piercing complaints! the dolorous lamentations! Oh, the groans, the sighs, the shrieks with which they shall fill each other's ears! One cries out, "Hot, hot, exceedingly hot!" Another cries out, "I am scorched, I am scorched, I am scorched all over! My feet, my hands, my head, all are burning!"

And all cry out, "Oh, dreadful, dreadful, dreadful day! Never did we see such a day as this; never did we see such smoke, nor feel such fire as this! Come help us, help us! Oh, someone please help us! Is there no one to pity? Is there no one to help or deliver? Will not God or Christ or angels or saints afford us any help? We cannot help ourselves; we cannot help each other; and the devils who have deceived us into this misery neither can nor would if it were in their power!

"But if we cannot shun it, let us try to see if we can quench it. Oh, come then; weep, weep, weep abundantly! Come, let thousands of us weep together, and drop our tears into one common place that we might pile up, and cast these waters upon some particular piece of ground whereby we may put out this burning fire. Though it will be but for a little while, perhaps we may find some rest and ease, some freedom from this pain.

"But, alas, what does it mean that we weep no faster? Our misery is great; our pain is great, our torment is exceedingly great; and our tears gush forth from our eyes, but we do not see them falling to the ground so that we might work, and cast them on the flames. Alas, alas, we now perceive that the tears are no sooner out of our eyes but the fire licks them off our cheeks. Though we weep abundantly, yet all our tears are dried up. This will not do! Alas, alas, woe is us, woe is us; this will not do! The fire burns; the fire burns faster and more fiercely for all the tears we have spent!

"Oh, come then, come away; let us go to some river or pond and cast ourselves therein; let us drown ourselves and die; better to die by water than bear the heat of fire. But, alas, we forget ourselves. We are now immortal and cannot die; if we could have died, this fire, this heat, this pain would have done it. But if we cannot die by water, let us fall into it and let it cool us. Though it does not kill us, it might ease or end our pain, though it cannot end our lives."

Oh, how they run; how they hasten to see who should get into it first. But, alas, the first there are the first to perceive this means to fail; for the ponds, the pools, the brooks, and all the rivers are dried up. There is not one drop of water left to cool their parched tongues, their scorched hands and feet.

So they cry, "Oh, come, then, come away; let us hasten to the sea, to the vast and mighty ocean. If there is any water to be had, it is there; if there is water to be had to quench this flame and ease our pained bodies, surely it is there! Oh, hasten, hasten! Do you not feel the drops of fire falling down on your backs from the melting heavens? Oh, which is the nearest way to the sea? He who is swiftest, run ahead; and then come and tell us what store of water yet remains!"

Remains? Alas, there is no hope; there is no remedy; the sea is dried up; the water is consumed; the whole ocean is licked up. Oh, now what consternation of spirit! What horror, what despair are they filled with now?

Brooks, rivers, seas, all dry? Oh, misery! What, have you gotten into such a fire and there is no water to be found? Not one bucket to be had? Oh, now, for some of those quarts and gallons of beer and wine you poured down your throats when there was no need! Oh, now, for some of those costly liquids with which you pleased your palates in the time of your prosperity in the world! Yea, no, the most dirty, filthy, nasty puddle water would be more prized than all your costly liquids before this.

But, alas, all this is but the beginning of their sorrows; it is vexing to these curious cowards, to these miserable souls, to see the beasts burning in this fire and dying by it. The beasts burn and are consumed; but these souls burn, but cannot burn into ashes. Fain they would do, but, lo, they cannot. They see the trees, the stones, the hardest metals burn, melt, and perish; but while they lived in the day of grace, their hearts were harder than the stones, and more resistant than the hardest metal. And now the fire that consumes and melts the one cannot consume or melt the other. They are tormented, but not consumed; they are pained in it, but cannot perish by it. Rather, they are reserved for another fire.

And now ten thousand devils come and seize upon them to draw them to another place, to a greater and more dreadful, lasting fire. To go from this into some shady place would be some ease and comfort to them; but to go from this into a worse place is enough to break their hearts, were it not that in that state their hearts cannot be broken.

But go they must, for the Judge has passed the sentence and commanded them to depart. Go they must, for the holy angels of God have gathered the tares and bound them in bundles, and are casting them into the fire. Go they must, for God has delivered them up to the executioners, to the devils in hell, who will drag them down into the everlasting fire, prepared for them and the devils together.

I cannot say that there shall truly be such actions, such running, such seeking water; for they shall know quickly that all such means have failed. I am only speaking according to our capacity to understand. It will be inconceivably more dreadful with the wicked when this world shall be in flames than these words or thoughts that I have used can set forth or declare.

See the inference which the apostle draws from the consideration of these flames which shall burn the world. 2 Peter 3:11, 14: "Seeing then that all these things shall be dissolved, what manner of persons ought ye to be in all holy conversation and godliness, beloved; seeing ye look for these things, be diligent, that ye may be found of Him in peace, without spot, and blameless."

Look to your state, that you be godly persons, that you be regenerate and have the image and likeness of God upon you. Such will be safe and out of the reach of the flames at that day; but woe be to the ungodly—they cannot escape.

Look to your conversation that it is holy, that you are holy in all manner of conversation (1 Peter 1:15). These great burnings, and the dissolution of all things, should take off your heart from the world, which ere long will be in flames, and quicken you to a holy and circumspect walking; that when the Lord appears, you may be found by Him in peace, without spot and blameless. And then you shall be taken to inhabit the new heavens and the new earth, those glorious mansions which the Lord will prepare for His people, where you shall have the presence of the Lord with you forevermore.

The third burning which will be is the burning of hell, which is the next discourse.

Fire and Brimstone

Part Three: In Hell to Burn the Wicked

Chapter 1

Introduction

The flames and fiery streams which were rained down from heaven upon Sodom and Gomorrah formerly, and which issued forth from the earth in the eruptions of Mount Etna lately, are but shadows of the future flames, and like painted fire in comparison to the streams of fire and brimstone which in hell shall burn the wicked eternally. The glory of heaven (while we are in the dark vale of this world) far exceeds all conception, and therefore cannot be set forth in full by any description; but, as one has said, "Whoever attempts to speak of a heavenly state while upon the earth, his discourse must be like the dark dreams and imaginations of a child concerning the affairs of this world, while yet swaddled and cradled in the womb."

The Apostle Paul himself, though he had been rapt up into the third heaven, and had such discoveries made to him there that he lacked words to utter what they were (2 Corinthians 12:2–4), yet acknowledged that he understood like a child, and had but dark views of this glory, even as through a glass (1 Corinthians 13:11–12).

So also, the torment of hell through that fire and brimstone which shall burn the wicked is beyond all thought to imagine or words to express. And when we have strained our conceptions to the highest pitch, when we have made use of the most dreadful and tremendous things that ever came to our eyes or ears, or in any way to our understanding, to help us form notions to ourselves of the horrible punishment which the damned shall endure in the unquenchable flames of hellfire, all falls beneath and far short of the reality. All our views hereof, by any representations, are like our sight of colors in the night: if not in whole, yet in the greatest part, they fly from our sight and disappear.

Yet since we are capable of understanding such future things only by shadows and representations, and since nothing can represent future burnings in hell as well as the greatest burnings that we may have seen upon the earth, therefore we may receive some help, by relating Sodom and Etna's storms and streams of fire and brimstone, to conceive something of those whereby the wicked in hell shall eternally be tormented.

DOCTRINE: God will rain a horrible tempest of fire and brimstone upon the wicked in hell as their deserved portion.

In treating this great subject I shall show:

First, that there is such a place as hell where the wicked shall be tormented.

Second, it is a place of fire and brimstone.

Third, what the properties of this fire are.

Fourth, who the persons are who shall eternally

burn in these flames.

Fifth, what the reason is for the eternal torment of the wicked by these flames.

Sixth, and last, I shall endeavor to apply this doctrine with some uses.

Chapter 2

*There Is Such a Place as Hell Where
the Wicked Shall be Tormented*

The blind heathen were persuaded of the existence of a place of torment, for however ignorant they were of Christ and His first coming to redeem the world, His resurrection, and His second coming to judge the world, yet, by the light of nature and reasoning from there, they arrived at an understanding of a Deity who was both just and good, that the soul was immortal, and that both rewards and punishment were prepared for the souls of men after this life, according as they were found either virtuous or vicious. And therefore, as they feigned such a place as Elysian Fields, where the virtuous should spend an eternity in pleasure, so also a place called Tartarum, or hell, where the vicious and impious should be eternally tormented. This Tartarum the poets set forth with many fictions to frighten people from vicious practices. Some of these are the four lakes of Acheron, Styx, Phlegethon, and Cocythus, over which Charon wafted over departed souls in his boat; the three judges Aeacus, Minos, and Rhadamanthus, who were to call the souls to account and judge them as to their state; Cerberus, the dog of hell with three heads, that would let none come forth once they were in; and several sorts of punishments inflicted:

iron chains, horrid stripes, gnawing vultures, wheels, rolling great stones, and the like.

Take part of Virgil's description of this place, which he feigns Aeneas to have visited:

> This way to Elysium leads, where such do dwell
> As have lived virtuously, th'other leads to hell,
> Where wickedness is punished. Aeneas' eye
> Turns quick unto the lefthand rock
> And there doth spy.
>
> Great structures closed in with triple walls about,
> This compas'd by Tartarian, Phlegethon throughout,
> With fierce and fiery streams, with noise like stones on
>   shore
> Rolled by waves of sea. On th'threshhold of the door
> Which lets into the place Tisiphona doth sit
> Awake, both day and night to watch and look to it,
> Girt with red pall. Here he did hear the noise of
>   chains,
> The sound of cruel lashes, th'groans and cries from
>   pains
> Which they endured within . . .

Although most of these things which we may find in many poets, and other heathen authors, are fictions of their own brians, yet that there is such a place as hell is real, and the punishments are real, and far beyond whatever any of the heathens could imagine it to be. Therefore let us consult the Scriptures, which will give clearer light in this thing, where God, who has made and prepared hell for the wicked, has made known the thing, and threatened to punish the wicked there everlastingly.

Look into the Old Testament. Psalm 9:17: "The wicked shall be turned into hell, and all nations which forget God." I know that the original word for "hell" signifies "the grave," but here it must have a further significance than that of the grave, since it is appropriated to the wicked, and such as forget God. Otherwise, it might as truly be said that the righteous shall be turned into hell, and those who remember, fear, love, and serve God, for they shall be turned into the grave. Isaiah 14:12–13, 15: "How art thou fallen from heaven [speaking here of the king of Babylon], O Lucifer, son of the morning! Thou hast said in thine heart, 'I will ascend into heaven, and exalt my throne above the stars of God'; yet thou shalt be brought to hell, to the sides of the pit."

That hell in this passage is not to be understood of the grave only, but also of the place where the wicked shall be tormented, will appear if you compare this place with Isaiah 30:33 where the prophet, speaking of the same king of Babylon, said, "Tophet is ordained of old, yea, for the king it is prepared; he hath made it deep and large, the pile thereof is fire and much wood; the breath of the Lord, like a stream of brimstone, doth kindle it." This description is applicable unto no place but that place of everlasting burnings which the Lord has prepared for the wicked. Indeed, Tophet was a real place upon the earth where some idolatrous Israelites offered up their children in sacrifice to Molech; but here hell is called "Tophet," alluding to that place because of the shrieks and cries which the damned shall make there, worse than the children did in Tophet when they were sacrificed by their cruel parents.

In the New Testament it is most clear that there

is such a place as hell prepared for both the soul
and body of the wicked to be tormented in. Matthew
5:29–30: "And if thy right eye offend thee, pluck it
out and cast it from thee, for it is profitable for thee
that one of thy members should perish, and not that
thy whole body should be cast into hell. And if thy
right hand offend thee, cut it off and cast it from
thee, for it is profitable for thee that one of thy
members should perish and not that thy whole body
should be cast into hell." That this "hell" does not
mean the grave into which the body shall be thrown
is evident because those who do cut off the right
hand and pluck out the right eye which offends
(that is, those who mortify those offensive lusts
which are as dear and difficult to be parted with as if
they were members of the body) shall be exempted
and delivered from this hell, whereas none shall be
exempted, though never so holy and mortified, from
the grave.

Yea, and in this hell it is said that both soul and
body shall be destroyed. Matthew 10:28: "Fear not
them which kill the body, but are not able to kill the
soul; but rather fear Him which is able to destroy
both soul and body in hell." Now the soul is not destroyed with the body in the grave, as they shall both
be, if wicked, after the resurrection in hell.

Moreover, this hell threatened by our Savior to
those who don't cut off right hands will appear
plainly to be the place of torment prepared for the
wicked by the description of it which is repeated
three times in Mark 9:43–48: "To go into hell, into
that fire which never shall be quenched, where their
worm dieth not, and the fire is not quenched." By

the unquenchable fire we are to understand the fire which shall burn the body; by the never-dying worm, the worm of conscience which shall eternally gnaw at the soul.

This hell is called a prison in 1 Peter 3:19–20: "By which also He went and preached unto the spirits in prison, which sometime were disobedient, when once the long-suffering of God waited in the days of Noah." By "the spirits in prison" we are to understand the souls in hell, the souls of those wicked and disobedient persons in the old world who would not give ear to the preaching of Christ by His Spirit in Noah; and therefore a whole world of them was sent into the prison of hell together, unto whom are gathered the souls of all who have since died in their sins where they are bound up in chains of darkness and reserved unto the judgment of the great day.

Hell is also called a "place of outer darkness, where there is weeping and wailing and gnashing of teeth" (Matthew 25:30). It is called a "furnace of fire," where all those who offend and do iniquity shall be thrown (Matthew 13:41–42). It is called "the great winepress of God's wrath," where all the wicked shall be crushed to pieces under the exceeding and eternal weight of His wrath (Revelation 14:19–20). But especially it is set forth as a place of fire, of which I shall speak in the next chapter.

Many divines have conjectured where hell is. Some have thought it to be in the bowels of the earth, because it is spoken of as a place below, and called by the name of "the pit," or the bottomless pit out of which the smoke and locusts did arise

(Revelation 9:2–3), and in which Satan was bound and held as in a prison (Revelation 20:1–7). And they have imagined that the pit spoken of in Numbers 16:33—into which Korah, Dathan, and Abiram went down alive when the earth was cleaved asunder and swallowed them up—was the pit of hell into which both their soul and body together were immediately conveyed, and that which has rather established such in this opinion has been the vast quantity of subterranean fire which they imagine to be in the bowels and caverns of the earth. Others have rather thought it to be beyond this visible world (which will pass away at the last day), and removed at the greatest distance from the place which the righteous shall eternally inhabit.

But the Scripture being silent about this, whatever is spoken on the subject of where hell is must be only by conjecture. The Lord grant that none of us may know by experience. Our chief care should be that we may escape the punishment, and not to be inquisitive about that which the Lord has not thought fit to reveal. Let it suffice us to know that there is such a place as hell where the wicked shall be tormented.

Chapter 3

Hell Is a Place of Fire and Brimstone

Thee is nothing by which hell is so described in Scripture as by fire, and sometimes by fire mingled with brimstone. It is called "fire" in Matthew 3:10: "Every tree which bringeth not forth good fruit is hewn down and cast into the fire." It is called "hell fire" in Mark 9:47: "The better for thee to enter into the kingdom of God with one eye, than having two eyes to be cast into hell fire." It is called "a furnace of fire" in Matthew 13:42: "And He shall cast them into a furnace of fire." It is called a place where the wicked shall be "tormented with fire and brimstone" in Revelation 14:10: "And he shall be tormented with fire and brimstone, in the presence of the holy angels." And it is called "a lake which burneth with fire and brimstone" in Revelation 21:8: "They shall have their part in the lake which burneth with fire and brimstone, which is the second death."

I know that it is a great question among divines whether the fire of hell which shall burn the wicked will be a real fire or a metaphorical one. There are men of great fame who assert it to be metaphorical, and that because it is called a fire prepared for the devil and his angels, who cannot be hurt by a real fire; because the worm which never dies is metaphorically taken for the everlasting gnawing of conscience; or because the New Jerusalem is metaphorically described to be of pure gold, clear like glass, the foundations garnished with all manner of precious stones, and the gates of pearls (Revelation 21:18–19), and thus, by the same reasoning, they say the description of hell in Scripture is metaphorical.

However, those who thus affirm the fire of hell to be metaphorical are so far from lessening the torment hereby, which this fire will inflict, that they much the more aggravate it. That metaphorical fire, they say, will afflict more than if it were real fire; for as the glory of the New Jerusalem, that building of God made without hands, eternal in the heavens, far surpasses all metaphors whereby it is set forth (which are made use of only to help our understanding in imagining its glory), so also the pain and torture of the damned in hell will be more horrible and intolerable than if they were to be cast into Nebuchadnezzar's fiery furnace when it was heated seven times more than it was wont to be heated. The point is that the metaphor always comes far beneath the thing that it is used to set forth.

Others are of the judgment that hell fire will be real fire, it being so positively, so plainly, and so frequently asserted to be fire: fire with flames, fire which shall burn; because nothing brings greater pain than fire; because it is proper for the body to be tormented with some real, material substance. And when the Holy Ghost tells us that it will be real fire, why would He turn this fire into a metaphor which may tend to weaken our conceptions of its horror rather than to heighten them? And therefore, in answer to that great objection, that it is said to be prepared for the devils, they are ready to say that it shall be such fire as will not only torment the soul, but also devils too. God has power to make such a fire. The other metaphors are made use of but once; this fire is the almost constant expression in Scripture wherever hell is described.

I confess that I do not judge the answers here to be fully satisfactory. For however the souls of wicked men and women may, by sympathy with the body, be tormented by real fire, yet God having made devils to be wholly spirits which are wholly incorporeal, I don't apprehend how any fire or bodily substance can have any impression upon them. Fire, air, earth, and water are all the same things to them, and they are incapable of suffering by any of them. As water cannot drown them, so neither can fire burn them; as air cannot refresh them, so neither can fire afflict them.

Indeed, were the opinions of some ancient men true that devils have bodies, just more pure and refined, such as cannot be seen any more than the air, a real fire might be made so pure by God as to torment the devils. But I am altogether of the judgment that devils are wholly spirits; the Scripture asserts this fact, and I might give many reasons for it, but it would be too large a digression.

Moreover, the fire of hell, I believe, will be such as will immediately afflict the souls of the wicked, and not only by sympathy with the body, because otherwise the torture of the body would be greater from its immediate object than the anguish of the soul by sympathy when the soul's degree of

deserving punishment is greater, being more highly
guilty of sin than the body which is made use of only
as an instrument.

Yet I cannot be of the opinion that the fire of
hell will *wholly* be metaphorical for the reasons before given; therefore I judge that both the opinions
may be reconciled with themselves and the truth by
asserting that this fire of hell will be partly
metaphorical and partly real.

First, I think that the fire of hell will be partly
metaphorical, and that this also will be the most
grievous and tormenting—though not to the sense,
yet to the soul, and to the devils who can be tormented by no other fire. My meaning is that the fire
which will be metaphorical is to be understood of
the fierce anger and wrath of the sin-avenging God,
who Himself is called "a consuming fire" in
Hebrews 12:29. His anger is often expressed in
Scripture by the metaphor of fire.

So that everlasting fire which is prepared for the
devil and his angels, and for the souls of wicked
men and women (which will be accompanied also
with a real fire, prepared for their bodies), is the everlasting wrath of God which He has treasured up
against the day of wrath, when He will open and
bring forth those "treasures," and make immediate
impressions there upon all damned spirits. This will
burn *worse* than fire, and cause greater anguish to
the spirit than any fire can do to the senses.

Hence Hebrews 10:31 says, "It is a fearful thing to
fall into the hands of the living God." That is because the immediate strokes of God's vengeance,
which damned spirits shall fall under when He

takes them into His own hands to punish them in hell, will, above all things, be most intolerable. The apostle writes in 2 Thessalonians 1:9 that the wicked shall be punished "with everlasting destruction from the presence of the Lord, and from the glory of His power." This is to be understood causally, as if he had said, "The destruction of the wicked shall arise from God's presence and glorious power, which will put itself forth so mightily as to glorify itself in the punishment of them in hell."

God will appear in heaven to the angels and saints in a flame of love, and make immediate and most sweet impressions thereof upon them, which will be their chief happiness. And God will appear in hell to devils and damned spirits in a flame of wrath, as a consuming fire, and make immediate impressions of His wrath upon them, which will be their chief misery. For sinners to be taken thus into the hands of God, and be punished by the fire of His wrath, will be more dreadful than if the most furious creatures in the world were mustered up together and let loose upon them to tear them in pieces and devour them. If they were tormented with the most exquisite torments which could possibly proceed from any second causes, it would be no more than the biting of a flea or the prick of a pin in comparison to the immediate strokes of God's vengeance and the burning under the fire of His indignation.

Second, the fire of hell, I believe, will be partly real, meaning that fire whereby the body shall be afflicted. I judge that as the torture will be real, so the fire whereby it will be tortured will be real too. Of all the senses, the sense of feeling is most capable of being tortured and afflicted; and of all the objects of this sense, fire is most afflictive and painful. Therefore, God has appointed fire to be for the punishment of the body. Indeed, other senses will be afflicted too: the ear with hideous noises, shrieks, and yells from fellow damned sinners; the eye with fearful, ghastly, and horrible spectacles; the smell with suffocating, odious, and nasty stench, worse than that of carrion, or that which comes out of an open sepulchre. But the feeling will be most afflicted by the devouring and eternally burning fire into which the wicked shall be thrown.

I will not dispute whether this real fire of hell will be such as our culinary fire (I mean, the kind in our chimneys), which sometimes creeps into houses, and is of such great force as to burn down cities and seize upon any combustible matter in its path. This kind of fire will continue no longer than it is fed by such gross matter. Nor will I dispute whether it will be more purely elementary fire, such as philosophers affirm to be between the upper region of the air and the lower orb of the heavens, or whether it will be such fire as sometimes breaks forth out of the bosom of the earth at the mouth of flaming mountains, of which some think there are vast treasures below, beyond whatever appeared to the eye, such as those flaming and burning streams sent forth from Mount Etna of late

This, at least, will help us to imagine something of what the lake of fire and brimstone will be, whether it will be a fire created on purpose by God, sulphurous and stinking, but far beyond that which was raised upon the wicked of Sodom and Gomorrah, which of all burnings that have ever been in the world, I think, most likely represented the burnings of hellfire.

I shall not, nay, I cannot determine in this case, but am most inclined to think that this fire will be immediately created by God, differing from all fires that ever have been in its fierceness, which by the word of God's power will be made, and by the breath of His indignation will be kindled and kept alive to all eternity without any fuel to feed it, except the bodies of the wicked, which, though they shall be tormented by it, shall never be consumed by it.

Chapter 4

The Properties of Hell Fire

There are seven properties of hell fire: it will be (1) a great fire, (2) a dark fire, (3) a fierce fire, (4) an irresistible fire, (5) a continual fire, (6) an unquenchable fire, and (7) an everlasting fire.

1. The fire of hell, which shall burn the wicked, will be a great fire. We have seen some great fires which have burned many houses together, such as the one that took place in 1666, which burned down the greater part of London; but this fire of hell will be so great as to burn all wicked persons together. All the wicked will be in flames at the same time. The greatness of this fire is set forth in Isaiah 30:33: "Tophet is prepared of old; He hath made it deep and large; the pile thereof is fire and much wood; the breath of the Lord, like a stream of brimstone, doth kindle it."

"Tophet" signifies hell, the place where the damned shall be tormented. God has made it deep and large; the depths of the earth or the depths of the sea are nothing in comparison with hell. For those depths have a bottom, but this is called the bottomless pit (Revelation 20:1). It is deep and large, of vast capacity; it will be sufficient to contain all the sinners of the old world, and all the sinners of this world who have lived or shall live in every genera-

114

tion until the time of the world's dissolution. The pile thereof is fire and much wood. As much wood kindled makes a great fire, so this fire (though it has no real wood, but that which will be equivalent) will be very great, especially kindled by the breath of the Almighty. As the breath of the Lord kindled those showers of fire and brimstone which came down from heaven upon Sodom and Gomorrah, so the breath of the Lord will kindle those streams of fire and brimstone which shall be in hell.

2. Hell fire will be a dark fire. There will not be the least glimmering of light in that doleful place, which will add to the horror thereof. Hell is called "outer darkness" in Matthew 25:30, and "blackness of darkness forever" in Jude 13. There will be no light of God's countenance, not the least smoothing of His brow. His wrath will be poured forth without mixture into the cup of His indignation, which they must drink of (Revelation 14:10). There will not be the least light of comfort, nothing but weeping, wailing, and gnashing of teeth. There will not be the light of the sun, or of the moon, or even of a candle; and the fire itself will give no light. All will be dark and black: black devils, black bodies, black souls; and they may without light have perceptions of one another, as devils have now unto whom light is of no use; or, if there is a duskish light there to represent one another's rueful countenances, and other frightful spectacles, be sure there will be no refreshing light. There the damned will be in a place and state of darkness forever.

3. Hell fire will be a fierce fire. The fire of Sodom, of Etna, yea, of London in the day of its burning,

was fierce; but no fire burned so fiercely as hell's fire will do. The fire of God's anger and wrath will burn fiercely. Now it only smokes against sinners; then it will break forth into a flame. Tongue cannot express how fiercely the wrath of God will burn when hereafter it shall seize upon the ungodly. Psalm 90:11: "Who knows the power of Thine anger? Even according to Thy fear so is Thy wrath."

The power of the anger which any creature may have is finite and limited; it reaches no farther than the body. But "who knoweth the power of God's anger?" It is infinite and unlimited, and such as will reach the soul and most grievously torment it through its immediate impressions.

"According to Thy fear, so is Thy wrath." That is, according to the fear which we have of God. The wrath of man is not proportionate to the fear which we may have of it (we often fear what men can do more than they are really able); but the wrath of God is commensurate and proportionate to the greatest fears thereof. Yea, it far exceeds! God can inflict more than our fears are able to conceive, and that because of the infinite power of His wrath. God will hereafter make the power of His wrath known (see Romans 9:22), and how fiercely will it burn then!

The fire also, which will torment the bodies of the wicked, will be very fierce. It will be so fierce as to torment every part from the crown of the head to the foot, and every part in extremity, in the utmost extremity, and that beyond its present capacity to endure.

4. Hell fire will be an irresistible fire; all the power of hell with its combined forces will not be

able to make the least resistance against the fire of God's anger. Nahum 1:6: "Who can stand before His indignation? And who can abide in the fierceness of His anger? His fury is poured out like fire, and the rocks are thrown down by Him." Isaiah 27:4: "Who would set the briars and thorns against Me in battle? I would go through them, I would burn them together."

Briars, thorns, dried stubble, or chaff cannot resist a consuming fire; so neither shall the wicked be able to resist the fire of God's jealousy. And the real fire which has been prepared in hell for the body will burn with that fierceness so that it may master and prevail over all; none shall be able to resist its force; it will pierce through and through every part of the body. We read of the three children in Daniel who were preserved in the midst of the fiery furnace, so that not so much as the smell of the fire was upon their garments; but none shall be preserved from burning in this fiery furnace. Indeed, the wicked shall not be burned up and consumed, but shall be always burning. And this brings us to the fifth point:

5. Hell fire will be a continual fire. Other fires are sometimes in and sometimes out, but this fire will always be in—always burning without any intermission, always burning in the same high degree of intention. There will be no assuagements of the flames of God's anger, no abatement of the fire of hell; this fire will always be equally hot, and always hot in the highest degree.

6. Hell fire will be an unquenchable fire. Matthew 3:12: "He will burn up the chaff with unquenchable fire." Mark 9:44: "Where their worm di-

eth not and the fire is not quenched." Now the fire
of God's anger, before it breaks forth into so vehement a flame, may be quenched by the blood of
Jesus Christ; and the fire of hell may be prevented.
But hereafter it will be too late: no sacrifice will be
accepted then to appease God's wrath. And if all the
waters of the seas could be poured upon the flames
of hell fire, they would be unable to put them out.

7. Therefore, hell fire will be an everlasting fire.
Matthew 25:41: "Depart from Me, ye cursed, into everlasting fire, prepared for the devil and his angels."
Revelation 14:11: "And the smoke of their torment
ascendeth up forever and ever." This fire will be ever
burning, and the damned will be ever tormented
therein. Extremity and eternity are the two most bitter ingredients of the damned's torments; who can
set forth the eternity of the wicked's punishments in
hell fire?

This eternity is immeasurable; it is incompre-
hensible; all the rays of the sun may be more easily
comprehended in a small room, and all the waters
of the sea contained in a small nutshell, than
boundless eternity could be conceived by our finite
and shallow understandings. None have shadowed
eternity and set it forth better than those who have
shown how infinitely short all measures and numbers fall when they are applied to the space of eternity's duration.

One expressed himself thus on this subject:
Suppose that ten thousand years have passed, and
after that a hundred thousand million years passed,
and after that ten hundred thousand million millions of years passed, yet you would not have come to

the end of eternity; no, nor to the middle of eternity; yea, you are only at the beginning of it. Add to this number all the thoughts of men and angels, all the motions in every creature, all the grains of sand which would fill ten thousand worlds; gather all the minutes of time from the beginning of the creation of the world, then add all the numbers of arithmetic that could possibly be conceived—and all this is but the beginning of eternity.

How long will eternity last? *Always!* When will eternity end? *Never!* As long as heaven shall continue to be heaven, as long as God shall continue to be God, and as long as the saints shall be happy in their enjoyment of God, so long shall the wicked be tormented in the fires of hell. We may apprehend the everlastingness of this fire of hell, but we cannot comprehend it.

Chapter 5

The Persons Who Shall Burn Eternally
In the Flames of Hell

It is upon the wicked that the Lord will rain this horrible tempest of fire and brimstone in hell. All the workers of iniquity, all who live and die in their sins, must suffer the vengeance of eternal fire. These are the chaff which shall be cast into the unquenchable fire (Matthew 3:12). These are the goats that shall be condemned to everlasting fire (Matthew 25:41).

Look into a few places wherein the plain letter of the Scriptures shows this, and describes the persons who shall be the subject of everlasting torment in hell fire. Matthew 13:41–42: "The Son of Man shall send forth His angels, and they shall gather out of His kingdom all things that offend, and them which do iniquity, and shall cast them into a furnace of fire; there shall be wailing and gnashing of teeth." Romans 2:6, 8–9: "Who will render to every man according to his deeds; to them that are contentious, and do not obey the truth, but obey unrighteousness, indignation and wrath, tribulation and anguish upon every soul of man that doth evil, of the Jew first, and also of the Gentile." 2 Thessalonians 1:7–9: "The Lord Jesus shall be revealed from heaven with His mighty angels in flaming fire, taking vengeance on them that know not God and obey not the gospel; who shall be punished with everlasting destruction, from the presence of the Lord and the glory of His power." Take one place more among many that might be offered, and that is Revelation 21:8: "But the fearful and unbelieving, and the abominable, and murderers, and whoremongers and sorcerers, and idolaters, and all liars shall have their part in the lake, which burneth with fire and brimstone."

I shall speak more of the persons themselves when I come to the application, the doctrine being so well-known. And therefore I shall but briefly touch upon the reason why the wicked shall be eternally tormented in the flame of hell, and so come to the use, which I mainly intend.

The torment of the wicked in hell is a punishment; and therefore it has a respect unto sin, the guilt of which lays God under an obligation to inflict this punishment upon them. Sin is the violation of a holy and righteous law, and an offense of an infinite Majesty, whose justice requires satisfaction. And this He can receive in no other way from sinners themselves than by their undergoing the punishment of hell. Although this punishment is not infinite in regard to the quality, yet it is infinite in regard to its duration; and therefore the torments of the wicked shall have no end.

Chapter 6

Use of Examination

When you hear of Sodom and Gomorrah's burning, you might think this was done long ago and be unconcerned. When you hear of Etna's burning, you might think this was far away and be unconcerned. But when we come to discourse of hell's burnings, here you are all concerned. Those burnings are past; these are burnings to come. Those burnings were for a while; these burnings will be forever. The greatest part of the children of men will be cast into these burnings, and very few comparatively will escape.

Oh, what a vast number of all kindreds, nations, and languages will there be tormented in hell forever! What a vast number of professing Christians, yea, of professors of the gospel! You need to look to it that none of you are found in that number.

The dreadfulness of these everlasting burnings should stir you up with all solicitousness and utmost diligence to inquire whether you are in danger, and how you might escape.

Most men and women who live this day upon the face of the earth are in danger of being thrown into the flames of hell. The whole world may be divided into two parts: they are either those who are in a state of nature or those who are in a state of grace.

The former are many thousands of times greater in number, and the Apostle Paul tells us expressly that such are "children of wrath" (Ephesians 2:3), and "if children, then heirs" (Romans 8:17). The children of God are heirs of heaven; the children of wrath, who are also called "the children of the devil," are heirs of hell. Only those who are in a state of grace are in a state of salvation; they alone are free from all obligation to the punishment of hell, having an interest in Christ's satisfaction.

There are two ways in which all the sons and daughters of men may be found (Matthew 7:13–14). One is a narrow way that has a strait gate, and very few are found therein: it is the way of holiness, of self-denial, of mortification and gospel obedience. And though this is the way of life and salvation, the way to glory and honor and everlasting happiness, yet it has but few passengers; few take this course.

The other is a broad way, which has the greatest crowd and throng, although it leads to destruction. This is the way of sin, the way of profaneness, licentiousness, unrighteousness, and disobedience. This is the course of the world. This way has a wide gate, and many go in there. And the reason our Savior gives is that the other way has such a strait gate, because of the difficulty of its passage, namely the wicket of regeneration. Few attempt to go through this strait passage; or, if they attempt it, they are quickly discouraged with the difficulty and so let it alone and take the broader way. They take the easier way of sin, the steps of which will certainly take hold of death and hell.

I beseech you all, with the greatest seriousness, to

examine yourselves and see whether you are in a
state of nature or a state of grace. You have all been
born once, but have you been born again? You have
been born of the flesh; have you been born of the
Spirit? You have borne the image of the earthly
Adam, but have you borne the image of the heavenly
Adam? You are partakers of the human nature; are
you partakers of the divine nature? Have you new
and clean hearts? Are they changed? Do you lead
new and holy lives? Are they reformed?

I beseech you to examine which of the two ways
you are walking in. Is it the broad way of sin and
wickedness, or is it the narrow way of faith and holiness? These are questions of great importance to
be resolved; your everlasting weal or woe, your salvation or damnation depends on them. If you are
brought into a state of grace, and have gotten in
through the strait gate into the narrow way, happy
are you that you were ever born. You shall not perish
with the wicked, but shall most assuredly attain
eternal life and glory.

But if you are in a natural state, if you are on the
broad way, and continue therein to the end of your
lives, you are undone men and women. Woe to you
that you were ever born. Heaven will be shut to you
and hell will be opened to you, where you shall be
inconceivably and eternally tormented in the flames
of that eternal fire.

Take heed that you do not err regarding your
state and way; thousands have gone to hell because
of such a mistake. It is very easy to err; it is difficult
not to err, and no mistake is worse than this mistake. All is not gold that glitters; all is not grace that

has the show of it; all are not on the way to heaven who pretend to it; many deceive others much and deceive themselves much more.

Nothing is more likely to effectually hinder you from attaining grace than ungrounded conceits that you already have it. If you nourish in yourselves a false faith and false hope, they would be so far from saving you that they would fasten you the more tightly in Satan's chains, whereby he will more imperceptibly and inevitably drag you into hell.

And think, if you go out of the world under a mistake, with fair but groundless hopes of heaven, and find yourselves unalterably judged by God to hell, how will this render the loss of heaven more bitter, and the pains of hell more grievous; think of the disappointment of happiness, especially such great happiness, and to be overtaken with misery, espcially such great misery, and that when all other measures are cut off forever of attaining the one or avoiding the other. These would be unspeakable vexations!

And let me tell you, it is better to be mistaken on the other hand than on this one. It is better to fear when you are gracious than to hope when you are ungracious. A dangerless fear is better than a fearless danger. The former may cause you to go droopingly for a while towards heaven; the latter will cause you go merrily, securely, and surely to hell.

I need not spend time in telling you that idolaters, adulterers, drunkards, swearers, blasphemers, scoffers of religion, persecutors of God's people, thieves, murderers, liars, apostates, profane persons, and all the more notorious workers of iniquity shall have their part in the lake "which burneth with fire and brimstone." And if any of you reading these lines are among these, and your conscience, upon even a slight reflection, accuses you herein, give me leave to hold you by the arm a little and ask you, "Why so fast? What does this haste mean? Why are you so furious? What does this eager pursuit of lust mean? Do you know whom you serve? And what do you think your wages will be? Do you know what is before you? Do you see the end of a sinful course? Do you know what hell is? Is it desirable to dwell with devouring fire? Do you think to escape in this way?" But the awakening use comes later.

But let me beseech you who are more sober and profess religion to examine your state. Take heed that you do not deceive yourselves, and thereby undo yourselves irrecoverably. Have you been under conviction of sin? And have these been followed with contrition, and that backed with sound humiliation, such as has rendered sin above all things most odious, and yourselves of all other persons most vile in your own eyes? Have you had conviction of Christ's righteousness? And has this worked hungering desires after Him? Are these accompanied with faith that brings you to Christ, choosing Him as most precious and needful for you, casting yourselves upon Him and renouncing your own righteousness, accepting Him and His righteousness, resigning yourselves up to Him, putting your neck under His yoke? Have you received the Spirit, enabling you to pray, mortifying sin, and quickening you unto all the duties of new obedience? Hereby you may know the changes of your state.

If your hearts remain unhumbled and unbroken for sin; if you are strangers to the work of faith, and have never truly closed with Jesus Christ; if you are without the Spirit of Christ, and are under the reigning power of any sin; if you live in the neglect of secret and public prayer, and of the great salvation which the Lord Jesus has purchased; if you have a form of godliness, but are without the power thereof, you will be found to be foolish virgins at last. You will have no admittance to the bridal chamber. You will be found to be hypocrites, whose portion is the burning lake; and it will be impossible for you to escape the damnation of hell. Hebrews 2:3: "How shall we escape if we neglect so great salvation?"

Chapter 7

Use of Admiration at the Security of the Wicked

Are the burnings of hell so certain, being threatened by God? Are they so dreadful, beyond any burnings that have ever been, both in regard to fierceness and duration? And are they indeed prepared for the wicked, and all graceless, Christless persons as their deserved portion? And are most of the children of men wicked, ungracious, unrighteous, unregenerate believers who are already condemned to this place of torment (John 3:18), and, by consequence, while such, every moment in danger of being dragged forth to execution? Here, then, we may sit down and wonder at the senselessness and carnal security of such persons, especially of those who sit under the light of the Word, which makes discovery of all this most plainly to them. Whatever their danger is, whatever their sins which have deserved hell, whatever God's threatenings of everlasting burnings, whatever execution there is and has been upon sinners like themselves, yet they are without any fear. They are fast asleep in sin and are very secure.

Though their consciences are full of guilt, their hearts full of lust, and their lives full of sin; though their steps are carrying them forward in the broad way which leads to destruction; though death has them upon the chase and is at their heels; though the wrath of God pursues them hard and is at their backs; though the day wherein they must give an account and be punished for their iniquity hastens greatly; and though the Judge stands at the door, yet they do not care. They do not fear; none of these things moves them; none of these things troubles them. They eat, drink, sleep, buy, sell, plant, build, and go on in a sinful course as if they will live here eternally, or as if their soul would perish with their body. They act as if all the things foretold in the Word concerning future retributions were but mere fables.

1. Some are this secure because of an atheistic persuasion that there is no God, because they are enemies to God and live in a course of rebellion against Him; and so it is their interest and desire that there should be no God. Therefore, they do what lies within them to work themselves unto this persuasion. There are too many in our age who endeavor to tear all sentiments of a deity from their minds so that they might sin freely without any checks or controls; that hereby they might arm themselves against the thrusts and wounds which the sword and arrows of God's threatenings would otherwise give them; and that by this means they might still the noise of their clamorous and accusing consciences, which otherwise would give them no rest under such heaven-daring provocations as they are guilty of daily.

But such persons, if they will not believe the engravings of God which are upon the face of the universe, and the impression of infinite power and an invisible Deity on His works which are visible to the eye, shall not remain long under their atheistic apprehensions. But He will make them know and feel that there is a God by the immediate impressions of His wrath upon their souls, and the dreadful flames of hellfire which His breath will kindle to burn their bodies everlastingly.

2. Others are secure, notwithstanding their danger, through a fond persuasion that there is no hell; that there is no account to be given, no judgment to be passed, no punishment to be endured after this life. They rather fancy that death puts a total end to their being, and that forever.

Such reason like this: "Our life is short, and in the death of a man there is no remedy. Neither was there any man ever known to return from the grave. For we are born out of nothing, and we shall hereafter be as though we had never been; for the breath in our nostrils is as smoke, and a little spark in the moving of our heart after which, once it is extinguished, our body shall be turned into ashes and our spirit shall vanish as the soft air. But life shall pass away as the trace of a cloud, or like a mist driven by the beams of the sun. Our time is a shadow that passes away, and after our end there is no returning; for it is firmly sealed that no man comes again."

Hence they are secure, and encourage themselves in wicked and licentious practices: "Come on, therefore; let us enjoy the good things that are present. Let us fill ourselves with costly wines and ointments. Let no flower of the spring pass us by. Let us crown ourselves with rosebuds before they are withered. Let none of us go without his part of our voluptuousness, for this is our portion and our lot."

Such persons live like beasts, and would persuade themselves that they shall die like beasts; that there is no immortality of the soul; that there will be no resurrection of the body, and, by consequence, no punishment of both in hell. In contrast, right reason will evince that the soul, being a spiritual substance, will survive the body, which the wiser heathens have acknowledged. Scripture clearly reveals this, and that the body shall be raised again at the last day, and that both the soul and the body of the wicked will be eternally tormented in hell. Scripture being the Word of God, no carnal reason could ever disprove these things; they are as certain as God is true.

3. Others, if they have not drunk in those atheistic and anti-Scriptural persuasions with which some are besotted and intoxicated, are yet secure and senseless of their danger through their ignorance or misapprehensions of God. They conceive Him to be made up all of mercy, that there is no fury in Him; that however sinful they are or have been, God is more merciful, and nothing is easier than to obtain a pardon from Him as long as they call on His name and cry for mercy, even though it is at their last gasp, no matter how wicked their lives have been. They believe they will be saved, not considering that God is also holy and jealous, just and righteous, as well as merciful and gracious. Such as go on still in their trespasses have no share in His mercy or in any of His promises.

4. Others lull themselves to sleep upon a bed of security because of their own and others' immunity,

thus abusing God's patience and long-suffering, which should lead them to repentance (see Romans 2:4–5). Because sentence against their evil works is not speedily executed, therefore their hearts are fully set in them to do evil and they are secure (Ecclesiastes 8:11). They do not consider that though God is long-suffering, yet He is not ever-suffering; that patience which they have long and greatly abused will at length break into fury. They do not consider that God's vengeance, though it has heels of lead, yet has iron hands; and though the fire of God's anger is long kindled, yet it will be longer, yea, forever burning.

5. Others quiet themselves for the present, and arm themselves against fears of hell, through their intent to repent and reform later. However much they indulge themselves for a while in their sinful course, yet they resolve shortly to become new men and women, to turn over a new leaf and lead a new life, and to become as holy and strict as the best. They do not consider that repentance is not in their own power, or that they provoke God hereby to deny grace to them hereafter, and to remove from them the means of working it. They do not remember how many thousands have perished with such intentions, which were never put into practice.

6. Others are quiet and secure through lack of serious consideration what their guilt and danger is. They fill up their time to the full with worldly business and secular employments, so much so that they leave themselves no room or leisure to think of sin and their near-approaching death, or of future wrath and the eternal burnings of hell of which they

are in danger. The cares of this world and the deceitfulness of riches choke their meditations in the first springing forth of them, so that no fruit comes from them which reaches perfection. If guilty sinners were to sit down for a quarter of an hour every day, and look upward to the angry God who frowns upon them; and then look down to the flames of hell which He is preparing for them; and then look forward to the last judgment, when they will be sentenced by the Judge to dwell with devouring fire and inhabit everlasting burnings; and if they were persuaded that if they continued in sin they could by no means escape—surely they could not be so secure!

7. Others are secure, though they are going on in the way of sin which leads to death and hell, because most of the children of men are going on in the same course. And they hope they shall fare as well as the others. Their forefathers trod in these steps, and their neighbors are their companions in sin, and if they are punished at last in hell they think they shall have enough company and bear it as well as others. They do not consider how intolerable the wrath of God is, and that their company in hell will be so far from alleviating their pain and torment that it will exceedingly heighten and aggravate it!

8. Others, yea, most, are secure through their frequent practice of sin. Custom in sin has taken away the sense of sin. Their lusts have enthralled and stupefied them. However conscience may have grumbled at first, especially when they first ventured upon some more notorious sins, yet now they have shut the mouth of conscience and have charmed and seared it as with a hot iron (1 Timothy 4:2).

9. Others are quiet and secure under their danger of hell because they are not as bad as others, because they do not run with others to the same excess of riot, and have escaped the more gross pollutions which are in the world through lusts. This is especially true if they carry some face of religion; if they have a form of godliness and employ themselves in all the outward exercises of devotion, and withal have had some inward flashy affections; if they have a counterfeit of all saving grace, though they were never truly humbled for sin, or emptied of themselves, cut off from the old stock, and truly, by faith, engrafted into Christ, and draw from Him all virtue and spiritual influence (which is proper to all those who are in Christ, and are free from condemnation through Him, as stated in Romans 8:1).

Thus the devil and the deceitful hearts of men bewitch and fool most in some of these ways, to still them in peace and security until destruction comes upon them suddenly, and that without remedy. And they are not awakened out of their spiritual slumber until they are awakened in the midst of the flames of hell.

Chapter 8

*Use of Reproof and Terror for the Awakening
of the Wicked and Ungodly Out of
Their Carnal Security*

How long will you sleep, O you sinners? How long will you slumber in such imminent danger, you graceless and Christless persons? What, sleep under the light? What, sleep upon the brink of the burning lake? Will nothing rouse you and awaken you out of this sleep? Are you resolved that it will prove the sleep of death? Shall it insensibly and effectually usher you to hell before you are aware? Have you been called already so long, so loud, so frequently, so fervently, and yet you deafen your ear? Have you been told so often of your guilt and danger, and yet harden your hearts? Will you yet hold fast to your sins, resolving not to let them go no matter what they cost you? Have your hearts been like so many brazen walls, beating back all the arrows of reproof and threatenings which have been shot at you? Or are they like clay and mud, which grow more hard and obdurate under the sun and light of the gospel which has shone upon you? Have no heavenly dews and showers of the Word yet melted and softened you, no fire and hammer remolded and framed you? Have you been threatened with death, wrath, and misery forever, and are yet not startled, yet stupid

135

and senseless?

Oh, that yet at length you might be awakened, and effectually persuaded by the Spirit of the Lord to lift up your eyes and look a little before you. Yonder! Yonder! Look, sinner, yonder! A horrible, burning tempest is driving towards you; a dreadful, burning lake is prepared for you; can you not see it? Look through the perspective of Sodom's burnings when fire came down from heaven, and Etna's burnings when fire came forth from the earth; and this will reveal something. But the perspective of the Word will show it more plainly. If you look upwards with this perspective, you may see some glimpse of the glory of heaven. And if you look downward with it, you may see some glimpse of the fire of hell.

Look, do you not see a horrible, deep, and large pit filled with horribly burning fire, and that fire filled with damned men and women? Lay your ear to the mouth of this pit, and hear what the dolorous complaints, what the shrieks and yells are of that cursed company! And do you not perceive yourself hastening forward in the way to this place of burning? And will you go forward still? Or will you allow yourself to be carried on furiously by your impetuous lusts until you have fallen into this pit, and there is no possibility of ever getting forth again?

But more particularly, I will lay before you some considerations to awaken the secure:

1. Think how doleful a day of trouble and adversity is likely to come upon you. If you are then in danger of hell, where will the quiet and security which now you have appear on that day? Possibly it may last and abide with you as long as the warm sun

of prosperity shines upon you. In the spring of youth and sensual delights, while you thrive and flourish in the world, while your friends and flatterers are around you, your health and outward peace remain with you; but you may live to see all your outward comforts lie dead before you, and hidden in the grave from your sight forever. Your sun of prosperity may set at the noonday of your lives; a black night of adversity may come upon you; stormy winds and a bitter cold winter of trouble and affliction may assault you, and wither all your sensual pleasures like the herb and flower of your field. Some unlooked-for providence may blast your estate and your name, bereave you of your dearest friends and relations, and withdraw all the fuel and provisions which you have been storing and laying up for your flesh and sensual satisfactions. However well and strong you are for the present, an unexpected sickness and death-threatening distemper may suddenly invade you and bring you down to the sides of the pit; it may fill you with such pain and grief as no outward enjoyments shall be able in the least to assuage.

And then think to yourselves, you who are in danger of hell, what dread is likely then to seize upon you like an armed man, which you will not be able to resist. Then your carnal security will fly away like a bird or a cloud, and vanish like smoke in the air. Then your false peace will be broken and torn to pieces, as the spider webs are by fierce winds, being utterly unable to resist the fierce blasts and rougher assaults of an adverse state. And, oh, how doleful and dismal is a day of trouble likely to be to you when all outward stays and comfort, all inward quiet and peace shall fail together; when there are storms abroad and worse storms at home, great trouble without and greater trouble within; when you shall fall under the scourge of outward affliction, and under the lashes of an accusing conscience. The fear of hell and everlasting burnings are likely to be more lively and afflictive in a day of trouble than when prosperity restrains conscience from doing its office.

2. Consider that if you should escape the greater storms of outward affliction in your life, yet you cannot escape the stroke of death. And think how the apprehensions of future wrath and burnings are likely to consume you with terrors at your latter end (Psalm 73:19). Death has a grim aspect, and looks with a fierce countenance upon guilty souls. And when this enemy assaults and wounds you; when your sickness comes and proves mortal to you; when the physician shall give you over and leave you, and your friends shall mourn and stand weeping around you; when death has seized upon the extreme parts of your body, and the cold, clammy sweats are upon you; when you apprehend the second death to be near, which will immediately follow upon the first death; when you think that while friends are conveying your body to your grave, devils shall drag your soul to hell—how are you then likely to awaken in horror, despair, and utter confusion!

The dying sobs and groans of some guilty sinners, when awakened at their entrance at the port of death, are dreadful; but the inward anguish of the heart is beyond all compass of conceit or expression of tongue.

3. But think how fearful the separation of your souls and bodies will be; think with what dread your spirits will appear before God, when your consciences shall furiously charge you with the guilt of all the sins which you have ever committed, and you have not one pardon to show nor one word to answer for yourselves. Being examined and accused and found guilty, you will be condemned unto eternal punishment. And think what your horror is likely to be then!

4. Think of the day of doom, when the Lord Jesus shall come. I mean, when He shall come down from heaven to judge the world; when the graves shall be opened, and you are called forth to appear before Him; when the book of your conscience shall be opened and all your sins made manifest to the whole world; when you, having nothing to answer, shall be sentenced to everlasting fire. "Depart from Me, ye cursed, into everlasting fire, prepared for the devil and his angels." When the Lord shall drive you out of His presence into hell, oh, what will your shrieks and outcries be on that day! (See my book, *Christ's Sudden and Certain Appearance to Judgment* [reprinted by Soli Deo Gloria].)

5. Think of the punishment of hell itself which you will be condemned to: what will there be taken from you, what will there be denied you, and what will there be inflicted upon you.

First, think of what will be taken from you in hell. All your riches will be taken away: riches will then take the wind and be gone, and you shall never set your eye upon them any more. You shall never buy and sell and get gain any more; never purchase

houses or lands, never inherit anything; never have
enough land to set the soles of your feet upon. All
your money and estate will perish with you, and, oh,
how poor and miserable will you perceive yourselves
to be then, when you are deprived of all your riches
and treasures on earth, and instead thereof are
made to possess treasures of wrath!

Your honor will also be taken away, and everlasting shame and contempt will be poured upon you.
Although you may be raised to a higher seat than
the ordinary rank now, then you must stand upon
even ground with the lowest person, such as whom
you would scorn to set with the dogs of your flock, or
to employ in the meanest office around you. The
crown will be plucked from your head, and the robe
will be torn from your back. All the honor of wicked,
great ones will be laid in the dust, and they will find
no more respect in hell than other men. Wicked
princes and noblemen, wicked knights and gentle-
men, will have no one to bow to them there and pay
them homage. The most highborn ladies who are
not born again (whatever they have here) will find
no courtship hereafter, but will be handled as
roughly as the lowest of their attendants.

All your sensual delights and pleasures will then
be at an end; they are now but for a season (Hebrews
11:25); yea, but for a moment (Job 20:5). Sometimes
they fail before life is at an end; be sure that hereafter they shall have an eternal period. In hell there
will be no feasting and delicious fare to pamper the
flesh, no carousing and drinking, no wine in bowls,
no chanting to the sound of the viol, no singing, no
dancing, no making merry. The glutton there shall

have no sweet morsels, the drunkard no sweet drafts, nor so much as a drop of water to cool and refresh him. The wanton shall melt no more in lascivious embraces. Nothing will remain of all your sweetness and pleasures here; there will be only bitter remembrances accompanied with unutterable grief and groans, and the intolerable sting and biting of the never-dying worm of conscience. Whatever you have prized and pleased yourselves with here, you will then be stripped of all; and, oh, how bitter will this be, to lose all that which you now so greatly esteem, and in which you place your chief happiness!

Second, think what will be denied to you in hell: you shall be denied admission into the kingdom of heaven. When you see Abraham, Isaac, and Jacob, and many from the east, west, north, and south coming to sit down in the kingdom of God; when you shall see all the saints of all ages shining like the sun, and caught up in the clouds to meet the Lord, and to be crowned by Him and received to inherit the kingdom prepared for them, you shall be shut out. No room will be found for you there. You could find no room for Christ in your hearts here, and He will find no room for you in His kingdom hereafter. The loss of heaven, of that unspeakable happiness which the angels and saints shall have in the immediate vision and fruition of God, when you come to understand what it is, will appear, as many observe, to be greater than the punishment of sense. This loss will especially be most grievous to you who have had discoveries and proffers of it, but have ne-glected and refused it, preferring some base lusts be-

fore it; oh, how will you then be ready to tear yourselves to pieces for madness and vexation!

Third, think what punishment in hell will be inflicted upon you: the soreness and intolerableness
of it, the sureness and unavoidableness of it, the
nearness of it, and the everlastingness of it.

Consider the soreness and intolerableness of it. Consider
both the pain which you shall feel in your bodies,
and the anguish which shall be put upon your souls.
If you are found among the wicked and ungodly at
the end, your bodies shall be tormented in every part
in the flames of hell fire. No pain is more grievous
now to the body than the pain of fire; but what is the
extinguishable fire on earth in comparison to the
unquenchable fire of hell? What is the fire of man's
kindling in comparison to the fire of God's kindling? What is fire fed by wood in comparison to fire
fed by the breath of God? No fire here can torment
like the fire which God has prepared for the bodies
of the wicked hereafter.

You have seen fiery ovens, and you have heard of
Nebuchadnezzar's fiery furnace. Should your bodies
now be thrown into such fires, you would find them
horribly painful; but the pains of hell fire will be a
thousand times more horrible and tormenting.
Your bodies cannot now endure much pain without
expiring, which puts an end thereunto; but hereafter God will strengthen your bodies to endure;
they shall have greater strength and quicker sense,
and so more capacity for pain, and they shall be
filled to the uttermost of their capacity.

Your bodies shall never die, and they shall be
filled with pain in the extreme, and that to eternity;

this will be very sore. All the tortures that were ever invented by the most mischievous mind, or executed by the most cruel tyrant on any whom they have had the greatest anger towards, are not so much as the least gentle touch in comparison to the torture which the least member of the damned shall endure in hell.

Some of you have had extreme pain in your heads; others have had extreme pain in your bowels; others have been extremely afflicted with pain in your legs; others have felt much torture with pain in your teeth. But if you live and die in sin, you shall be extremely and eternally tortured with pain in every part: your eyes shall be full of pain, your tongues full of pain, your hands full of pain, your heads full of pain, your bellies full of pain, your feet full of pain; from the crown of your head to the sole of your feet, no part shall be free. Your bodies shall roll and tumble in flames, and there burn with horrible pain and yet never be consumed.

But the anguish of your soul will far exceed the torture of your bodies; and here words fail and concepts fall short. Who can tell how the worm of conscience will bite? Who can tell how dreadful the lashes of your consciences will be when they are let loose, as God's executioners, with full rage upon you? Who can utter the anguish you shall endure under the immediate impressions of God's wrath upon your souls? This will exceed whatever can be inflicted by the means of any second causes. The punishment of hellfire will be very sore and intolerable. Such as are tender cannot, without unutterable fear and grief, bear the thoughts of being burned alive here on earth; and, oh, the shrieking of such persons when they have been brought to the fire and the flames begin to seize upon them: "I cannot endure it! I cannot endure it!" How intolerable then will hell fire be!

Many martyrs have endured great tortures in their bodies with much patience. Some were slain with the sword, some burned with fire, some scourged with whips, some stabbed with iron forks; some have had their skins plucked off while alive; some have had their tongues cut out; some have been stoned to death; some have starved with hunger and cold; some were dismembered and naked to the shame of the world. And yet, in the midst of all their pains, they have had a composed mind; yea, sometimes they have been filled with joy.

God has not suffered man to inflict upon these martyrs more than He has given them strength to bear; but there will be no patience to undergo the pains of hell. The spirit will utterly sink under the heavy burden and pressure thereof, especially the pressure of that pure and weighty wrath which shall be immediately upon the soul. The terrors of conscience here, and foretastes of wrath, are intolerable in this world. Proverbs 18:14: "The spirit of man will sustain his infirmity, but a wounded spirit who can bear?"

If the body is infirm and weak, full of distemper and pain, yet while the spirit is whole and sound, while there is peace within, the spirit may sustain this and bear up under it. But if the spirit is wounded by the arrows of the Almighty that have been shot into it, who can bear it? If God lets fall

some scalding drops of His wrath upon the spirit, if
He kindles a spark of hell fire in your conscience,
who can endure it? No balm or physician on earth
can cure such wounds; no earthly riches or sensual
delights can assuage these inward griefs and hor-
rors which, by the hand of God, are imprinted upon
the spirit. When the wicked are filled with disdain-
ful agonies, through apprehension of future ap-
proaching wrath, and there remains nothing but a
fearful looking for of judgment and fiery indignation which shall devour the adversaries (Hebrews
10:26–27), this is enough to sink the heart of the
stoutest person under its burden.

And if the wounds of the spirit here are so intolerable, what will those be which the Lord, with such
mighty force and by His immediate hand, shall give
hereafter? If you cannot bear some drops of God's
wrath now, what will you do when the full vials of
God's wrath shall be poured out upon you, if you are
found under the guilt of sin? If you cannot endure
the sparks of hell fire, how will you endure the
flames, and the burning heat thereof? If the foretastes of hell affect your heart with such horror, and
the fears thereof fill the spirit with such amazement,
what will hell itself do when the pains and anguish
thereof are beyond the greatest fears and highest
conceptions thereof?

Should you fall into the hands of the most cruel
men to torture and massacre you, this would be fearful; should you fall under the power of devils to tear
and rend you, this would be more fearful; but to fall
into the hands of God will be most fearful. This you
cannot bear, and yet if you are wicked you must bear

it, and that to eternity. And can you sleep still in sin
under the thoughts of such danger?

Consider the sureness and unavoidableness of hell fire.
Nothing is more sure than what God has revealed in
His Word, and nothing is more unavoidable than
what God has threatened; and such is the tormenting of the wicked and ungodly in the flames of hell
fire. While you are here upon the earth, there is a
possibility of escaping future torments. Pardon,
peace, and salvation are attainable if you lay your
sins to heart; if you confess and forsake them, you
may find mercy. If by faith you apply yourselves unto
the Lord Jesus, you shall not perish, but find eternal
life. But if you go on still in your trespasses, if you
live and die in a state of impenitence and unbelief,
it will be impossible for you to escape. Indeed, could
you make your party good against God, could you
gather forces together and wage war against heaven,
obtaining victory, you might avoid the threatened
punishment; but, alas, God is infinite in power, and
will not permit any such attempts. You will not be
able to hold up either your head or your hand
against Him. Who can stand in His sight once He is
angry?

God will bind all the devils and wicked men and
women together in chains of darkness, stronger
than any iron chains, and none shall be able to
make any resistance. If you could hide yourselves on
the last day from His eye; could you fly from His
presence into some remote corner; could you creep
under some rock or mountain, and there be covered
from His view, you might think to escape—but this
cannot be. God's eye will follow you, and His hand

will reach you wherever you go. Could you, by your prayers and tears, move God to compassion, and prevail for mercy, as now you may do, there might be some hopes of avoiding this punishment. But here-after God's ear will be shut, and the doors of mercy shut against you forever. Your knocking at the door will be in vain; it will never be opened; your cries and prayers will be to no purpose; they will receive no answer. Hereafter the punishment of hell will be unavoidable by the wicked.

Consider the nearness of this punishment of hell. The sands of your life are running swiftly; the time of your abode here is wasting very fast; your bodies will quickly be in the grave, and, if you die in your sins, your soul will be as quickly in hell. You cannot long escape this punishment. You may shuffle the thoughts of God and future wrath out of your mind for a time; you may busy your thoughts about other things while you are here; but all these things will shortly shrink away from you and leave you naked. You must stand before God to be judged by Him, to be condemned by Him, and to be punished by Him. God will meet you, as a bear bereaved of her whelps, and rend the inner parts of your heart, or as a roaring lion, and tear you in pieces, and there will be none to deliver you. God will take you into His hand and throw you out of His presence into the bottomless gulf of unquenchable burnings. I think this should awaken you.

Consider the everlastingness of hell fire. Consider the torment which you must there endure if you are found in the number of unbelievers. The wrath of God will never be at an end; the worm of your conscience will never die; and the fire of hell will never go out. But the smoke of your torment will ascend up forever and ever. When you have been the space of as many years in hell as there are stars in the firmament, as there are drops of dew upon the earth in the morning, as there are spires of grass which spring out of the earth, as there are drops of water in the ocean, as there are sands upon the seashore, your torments will be as far from being assuaged, and as far from being ended, as at the first minute of your entrance into this dreadful place.

As there is an infinite space of place (if I may so call it to help our apprehensions) beyond the circumference of the heavens and the visible world, in comparison with which ten thousand millions of worlds would not fill up the space of the least speck, so there is an infinite space of duration beyond the circumference and bounds of time in comparison with which the duration of ten thousand millions of worlds for ten thousand millions of years would not be so much as a minute or the least imaginable instant. And if you are wicked, you must spend this whole eternity in extreme torment; the real length of eternal torment cannot be measured, and the imaginary length will be greater (if I may so say) because of your misery.

If a short time of misery here on earth seems long, what will an eternity of misery seem to be in hell? When the body is in health and the soul is sweetened with delight, time steals away insensibly. Years seem to be months; months seem to be weeks; weeks seem to be days; and days seem to be hours. But when the body is sick and the soul is embittered with sorrow, a short time seems long, and it passes away slowly in our apprehension. Hours seem to be days, days weeks, weeks months, and months years. At those times, how we count the clock, and reckon that fall in the glass; time seems to have lead heels. How long, then, will the eternity of extreme misery seem to be?

I believe that the space of one quarter of an hour in hell will seem longer to the damned than a whole life of misery in this world. Yea, I think that a minute's pain in hell will seem longer to the wicked than a thousand years of pleasures in heaven will to the righteous, who will sweetly pass forward in the infinite duration of joy, without the least trouble or tediousness. So that the eternity of misery in hell will be, as it were, a double, triple, yea, thousand-fold eternity.

I think these considerations should startle all you who are asleep in sin. I think they should make your hearts quake, and every joint tremble. I think sinners in Zion should be afraid, and fearfulness should surprise the hypocrite. I think I should hear some of you cry out what we read in Isaiah 33:14: "Who among us shall dwell with devouring fire? Who among us shall inhabit everlasting burnings?" You should cry out as did the jailer in Acts 16:29–30, when awakened by the earthquake and the impression of guilt made by God upon his conscience, "Sirs, what shall we do to be saved?"

Chapter 9

Use of Comfort to the Righteous

Such of you as are righteous through the perfect righteousness of Christ made yours by faith, without the imputation of which (because whatever righteousness you may have within you is imperfect) it is impossible that you should escape the damnation of hell. You who are clothed with the white robes of Christ's righteousness, under which all your iniquities are covered, and withal have the Spirit of Christ given to you to work you into a conformity unto the image of Christ in your regeneration and sanctification, which are inseparably joined to justification by faith—you may take comfort in this doctrine which is of such terror to the wicked and ungodly.

In Samson's riddle, out of the strong and fierce lion came both honey and sweetness. So this doctrine, which looks with such a fierce aspect upon those who are outside of Christ, yet will yield sweetness unto you who are in Him because "there is no condemnation unto them which are in Christ Jesus" (Romans 8:1), and because Jesus "hath delivered you from the wrath to come" (1 Thessalonians 1:10). Who shall lay anything to your charge when God has justified you? Who shall condemn you when God has acquitted you? Need you value the wrath of men when you are delivered from the wrath of God?

Need you fear men's threatenings of temporal punishment, which can reach no farther than the body, when you are delivered from condemnation to the eternal punishment of soul and body in the lake which burns with fire and brimstone? What if you should lose your estates? Since you are not in danger of losing your souls, what if you should be thrown into a prison on earth? Since you are not in danger of being thrown into the prison of hell, you may take comfort; and the consideration hereof may alleviate all your fears and grief upon the account of any pains and afflictions which in this life are upon you, or which you are in danger of.

You may say of them all, "These are not the torments of hell. These are light, the other heavy; these short, the other eternal."

Lift up your heads with joy then. Yet a little while and you shall see what a difference the Lord will put between you and the wicked. When they shall weep, you shall laugh; when they shall mourn, you shall be glad; when they shall cry and howl, you shall sing and leap for joy; when they shall go sighing to hell, with everlasting horror in their hearts, and all mirth and joy shall flee away from them forever, you shall come singing to heaven with everlasting joy in your hearts. And all sorrow and mourning shall flee away and never any more be found.

Chapter 10

Use of Exhortation to Both the
Wicked and the Righteous

And now, sinners, what will you do? Will you dare to go on in that broad way of sin, which ere long will open under you and let you down into the horrible gulf of unquenchable burnings? Can you be content with a portion in this life, and to receive all your good things here, and that fire and brimstone and everlasting burnings shall be the portion of your cup hereafter? Will any pleasure of the flesh, and sin for a season, countervail that everlasting pain and misery which will be the bitter fruit and consequence of them?

Let me therefore exhort you to come out of the broad way of sin without delay. It is the way of hell; and will you proceed any further in it? You who are profane and unclean, you who are swearers, Sabbath-breakers, scoffers of religion, persecutors of God's people, drunkards, covetous persons, yea, all you who are hypocrites, who are impenitent and unbelieving persons: give me leave to stop you in your course, or rather hearken unto the voice of God, who calls you to turn from your evil ways so that iniquity will not be your ruin.

Come out of the broad way and get into the narrow way. It has a strait gate, namely the gate of regeneration; this you must pass through. You must become new creatures, get new hearts, and lead new lives. You must walk in the narrow way of mortification, self-denial, and new obedience; otherwise you will certainly be numbered among the damned who will be everlastingly burned in the fires of hell. The passage is difficult and the way narrow, but both are necessary; for it is the passage from death to life, and the way from hell to heaven.

Nothing in the world is so absolutely necessary as that which is necessary unto salvation. Better that the belly be without food than that the heart be without grace; better that the back be without raiment than that the soul be without righteousness; better to be starved than damned; better to be hanged than burned; better to die the most painful, temporal death than endure the pains of eternal death.

But those of you who have passed through the strait gate of regeneration, and have gotten onto the narrow way, you are safe; you are on the way to heaven. Learn to admire free grace, which has made the difference between you and the most vile sinners. Endeavor to bring others onto the same way; commend to them the ways of God, both by your word and example, and persevere in those ways to the end of your life. Be faithful until death so that you may receive the crown of life.

I shall close this discourse with the words of the apostle in 1 Corinthians 15:58: "Therefore, my beloved brethren, be steadfast and unmoveable, always abounding in the work of the Lord, forasmuch as ye know your labor is not in vain in the Lord."

When the wicked are steadfast and immovable in the ways of sin, and no argument can persuade them to forsake those ways; when they abound always in the work of the devil, and the wages which they shall reap will be death, wrath, and everlasting burnings in hell—you be steadfast and immovable in the ways of the Lord. Do not be allured by flatteries, nor frightened out of them by threatenings, but abound more and more in the work of the Lord, and your reward shall be everlasting life and glory in heaven.

The Only Deliverer from the Wrath to Come

or The Way to Escape the Horrible and Eternal Burnings of Hell

"Even Jesus, which delivered us from the wrath to come." 1 Thessalonians 1:10

Past pains may easily be forgotten; future pains are not easily believed; present pains in extremity are so grievous and afflicting that all the wealth and honor in the world cannot countervail them. And, oh, how welcome is such a physician who can give ease and remove them! But if people believingly apprehended what horrible pains and torments the wicked must endure in the unquenchable flames of hell fire, where they can have no ease, and their misery shall have no end; if they apprehended how fearful a thing it is to fall into the hands of the living God, and to be swallowed up by His wrath, which pursues all who are out of Christ, and which will certainly come and may quickly seize upon them, surely they would use their utmost diligence now to escape—surely they would, with the greatest inquisitiveness, seek out a place of refuge from the fiery tempest of God's vengeance!

This text, which makes a revelation of the only Deliverer from the wrath to come, would sound with

most transcendent sweetness in their ears; and the
glad tidings thereof, concerning what Jesus has
done for His people, would, above all things, be
most welcome in their hearts. "Even Jesus, which delivered us from the wrath to come."

In the former verse, the apostle tells the
Thessalonians what manner of entrance he had at
first among them, and what the great effect of his
ministry was upon them, namely that they were con-
verted thereby, which conversion he sets forth:

1. By the nature of it: they were turned from dead
idols, the lying vanities which they worshipped and
served before, unto the living and true God, to worship and serve Him.

2. By the consequence of it, which was their waiting for the second coming of the Lord Jesus Christ
from heaven. And here he shows:

First, the evidence of this second coming: it will
certainly be, namely by God's raising Him from the
dead and receiving Him into heaven.

Second, the ground of their hope and comfort-
ing expectation, and waiting for this coming in the
text: because this Jesus had delivered them from the
wrath to come. The wicked, if awakened, look for
Christ's second coming with dread and fearful expectation because of the wrath which He will bring
with Him, because He will come in flaming fire to
take vengeance upon them. The righteous, if as-
sured of their interest in Christ, look for Christ's
second coming with gladness and joyful expectation
because He has delivered them from the wrath to
come. "Even Jesus, which delivered us from the
wrath to come."

The doctrine, then, is plainly set forth in the words of the text:

DOCTRINE: It is Jesus who delivers from the wrath to come.

In handling this point I shall show:

1. What this wrath is which is to come;
2. That this wrath is to come;
3. Upon whom this wrath will come;
4. When this wrath will come;
5. Who this Jesus is who delivers from wrath to come;
6. How Jesus delivers from wrath to come;
7. How any do or may have a share in this deliverance by Jesus from wrath to come;

Then I shall make some use and application.

1. What this wrath is which is to come.

It is not the finite wrath of the most furious and fierce creatures; it is not the wrath of lions, bears, tigers, wolves, or wild bulls; it is not the wrath of the most potent and tyrannical men, who may exceed all these in ferocity and cruelty. Neither is it the wrath of the devil, whose wrath is great here on earth when let loose to tempt and deceive, but most furiously will express itself hereafter in hell when he is let loose as God's executioner to torment the wicked. But by "the wrath to come" we are to understand the infinite wrath of the sin-avenging God, in comparison with which the wrath of all other creatures in the world is mild, and not in the least to be regarded.

We read in the Scripture of the wine of God's wrath (Revelation 14:10), that this wine is red (Psalm

75:8). We read of the vials of God's wrath (Revelation
16:1), of the cup of God's wrath (Revelation 14:10), of
the winepress of God's wrath (Revelation 14:19). We
read of the treasures of God's wrath (Romans 2:5), of
the vessels of God's wrath (Romans 9:22). By "the
wine of God's wrath" we are to understand those
plagues and punishments which God does and will
inflict upon the wicked for their sins. By "the red-
ness of the wine" is meant the dreadfulness of those
plagues. By "the vials of God's wrath" we mean some
smaller plagues and temporal punishments on
earth. By "the cup of God's wrath" we mean
especially the dregs and bottom of it, the greater
plagues and eternal punishments of hell. By "the
winepress of God's wrath" we are to understand the
place where the wicked shall be punished. By "the
treasures of God's wrath" we are to understand the
abundance of plagues; by "the vessels of wrath," the
damned who are appointed to undergo these
plagues and torments. These vessels God will fill
with the measures of His wrath. He will fill them to
the brim in hell with the most exquisite torments.

And this is the wrath which is to come, which
will be most bitter, beyond any gall or wormwood to
the taste. This wrath will be most pure, without any
allay or mixture of any comfortable ingredients.
This wrath will be most plentiful, the treasures of
which will be opened in hell, and all the damned
will be filled with it abundantly. It will be most
weighty, beyond any mountain of lead, to sink sinners down into the bottomless pit. It will be most
fierce, and so powerful that all the powers of men
and devils shall not be able to make the least resis-

tance. It will be intolerable, and yet must be borne; it will be implacable, so as never to be appeased; and it will be eternal, so as never to be ended.

Plainly, the wrath to come is the same as the punishment of hell, the great effect of the wrath of God. This punishment has two parts: the punishment of loss and the punishment of sense.

The punishment of loss will consist of the loss of the crown, glory, and happiness of heaven, where the righteous shall be admitted to the immediate vision and full fruition of God the chief good, which will fill them with soul-ravishing, inconceivable, and eternal joy. But from this all the wicked will be eternally shut out, and wholly denied any share in the least of that happiness which, when they come to understand the worth and excellency of it, will above all things be most vexing to them.

The punishment of sense will consist in the horrible pains and tortures which shall in extreme measure be inflicted upon every part of the bodies of all the wicked by the most dreadful and unquenchable fire into which they shall be thrown, and the horrible anguish which, through the immediate impressions of God's wrath, shall be inflicted upon every faculty of their souls in hell, where they shall have no ease or release forever. Matthew 25:41: "Depart from Me, ye cursed, into everlasting fire, prepared for the devil and his angels." Revelation 14:10–11: "The same shall drink of the wine of the wrath of God, which is poured out without mixture into the cup of His indignation, and shall be tormented with fire and brimstone in the presence of the holy angels and in the presence of the Lamb.

And the smoke of their torment ascendeth up forever and ever, and they have no rest day or night." See more of this in my book *Christ's Sudden and Certain Appearance to Judgment,** and in the first part of this book *Fire and Brimstone.*

   2. This wrath of God is to come, which implies two things: the wrath is not yet come, and it certainly will come.

First, the wrath of God has not yet come. Had it already come, who could have stood before it? Who could deliver from it? Where it seizes, it crushes and it burns, and that worse than any fire. Where it seizes, it holds and never lets go its hold. But, as it has not yet come, some sparks of this fire may be let fall in temporal judgments upon sinners in this life; but what are temporal judgments in comparison to eternal ones? In this world, God exercises His patience towards the wicked. He is angry with them, and His anger smokes against them; but He withholds His wrath from breaking forth into a flame, which would quickly devour all the wicked of the earth should He give way to it and let it loose upon them. Indeed, we read in John 3:36 that the wrath of God abides upon unbelievers; that is, it shall abide upon those who at last are found in a state of unbelief as surely as if it already were abiding on them; or, the wrath of God abides upon unbelievers, that is, the sentence of condemnation unto this wrath abides upon them. John 3:18: "He that believeth not is condemned already." Indeed, it is said of the persecuting Jews who had killed the Lord Jesus and

---

* This book has been published by Soli Deo Gloria.

their own prophets, and had forbidden the apostles to preach to the Gentiles, that "the wrath was come upon them to the uttermost" (1 Thessalonians 2:15–16). But we are to understand it thus: the wrath of God was come upon them to the uttermost not in regard to eternal judgments, but in regard to spiritual judgments, it being the expression of God's wrath here to give sinners up to a persecuting spirit which prepares them for the uttermost and most dreadful punishments of hell hereafter. But as yet the wrath of God has not yet come; none in this world does or can know the power of God's anger.

Second, the wrath of God is to come, that is, it will certainly come; there are some things which may come, such and such temporal judgments may come, such and such deliverances may come, but there are some things which *will* come. Death will come, Christ will come, and, as certainly as death and Christ will come, so certainly this wrath of God will come. God has foretold it; and heaven and earth shall pass away, but not one jot or tittle of what God has foretold until it is fulfilled. God has threatened it, and God is not more faithful in His promises to His people than He is true in His threatenings to His enemies. God's justice engages Him to send it, which can be satisfied in no other way by those who have no interest in the satisfaction of Christ.

The wicked are vessels fitted by sin for destruction and prepared for wrath; and therefore they shall be filled with it, even as the vessels of mercy are fitted for and shall be filled with glory. God has treasured up wrath for the wicked as they have treasured up sin; and God will give them that which they have so much deserved, and which He has prepared for them. However sinners may escape this wrath for a while, and vainly hope to flee or hide themselves from the stroke of God's vengeance, yet God's right hand will find all those who hate Him; and He will make them as a fiery oven in the time of His anger, swallow them up in His wrath, and devour them with the fire of His indignation (Psalm 21:8–9).

3. Whom this wrath will come upon.

First, the wrath of God will come upon all the children of disobedience. Colossians 3:5–6: "Mortify therefore your members which are upon the earth, fornication, uncleanness, inordinate affection, evil concupiscence, and covetousness, which is idolatry; for which things' sake the wrath of God cometh on the children of disobedience." Such are children of disobedience who are disobedient children, such as do not yield obedience unto the law of God, but live in and allow themselves the practice of known sins, and the neglect of known duties; they are such as are under the power of reigning sin, who are willing servants of sin, who yield up their members as instruments of unrighteousness to sin (Romans 6:13), who serve divers lusts (Titus 3:3), and who make provision for the flesh, to fulfill the lusts thereof (Romans 13:14). They are such as are blasphemers, swearers, Sabbath-breakers, murderers, adulterers, drunkards, thieves, covetous, unrighteous, extortioners, revilers, scoffers at religion, persecutors of God's people, or who have an enmity to the power of godliness; such as are proud and boasters, such as are disobedient to parents without natural affection, such as are lovers of pleasure more than lovers of God, such as are liars and unfaithful, such as are idle and slothful, such as live in envy and malice, such as are given to revenge and cannot forgive injuries, and other like sinners—all children of disobedience upon whom the wrath of God will come. Ephesians 5:6: "Let no man deceive you with vain words, for because of these things cometh the wrath of God upon the children of disobedience."

Let none deceive you with vain words, neither deceive yourselves with vain thoughts, as if you might escape the wrath of God although you live in the practice of such and such sins. See how vain and groundless the security of such persons is. Deuteronomy 29:18–20: "Lest there be among you a root that beareth gall and wormwood; and it come to pass, when he heareth the words of this curse, that he blesseth himself in his heart, saying, 'I shall have peace, though I walk in the imagination of my heart, to add drunkenness to thirst.' The Lord will not spare him, but then the anger of the Lord and His jealousy shall smoke against that man, and all the curses that are written in this book shall lie upon him, and the Lord shall blot out his name from under heaven." Moreover, we read in Galatians 3:10: "Cursed is every one that continueth not in all things which are written in the book of the law to do them."

Such as are guilty of any transgression of the law (while out of Christ) are under the curse, and liable to God's wrath. Hebrews 2:2: "Every transgression and disobedience received a just recompense of reward." Hence it is that the children of disobedience are called children of wrath (Ephesians 2:2–3).

Second, the wrath of God will come upon all hypocrites; it is more peculiarly appropriated unto them as their portion. Matthew 24:51: "He shall cut him asunder, and appoint him his portion with the hypocrites; there shall be weeping and gnashing of teeth." Whoever escapes God's wrath, hypocrites shall not escape; whoever is pardoned, hypocrites shall be punished: such as have a form of godliness, but deny the power thereof; such as make some outward show of reformation, but are without inward transformation; such as are like painted sepulchres, fair and beautiful without, but within are full of rottenness; such as make it their great business to appear religious, and take no care to be religious, but are rotten at heart and cover carnal designs with a cloak of profession. As their sin is most offensive unto God here, so His wrath will certainly come upon them with the greatest severity hereafter.

Third, the wrath of God will come upon all impenitent and unbelieving persons. Luke 13:3: "Except ye repent, ye shall all likewise perish." Mark 16:16: "He that believeth not shall be damned." Repentance and faith are two great duties of the gospel, and wrath is particularly threatened to such as do not obey the gospel; to such God will render indignation and wrath, tribulation and anguish (Romans 2:8–9). And Christ will come in flaming fire to take vengeance upon them (2 Thessalonians 1:8). Such as are impenitent and unbelieving neglect the salvation of the gospel which, by faith in Christ alone, is attainable; sinning against the only remedy, they cannot escape. Hebrews 2:3: "How shall we escape if we neglect so great salvation?"

4. When this wrath of God will come.
First, the wrath of God will come in part upon
the wicked immediately, after the separation of their
souls from their bodies. The souls of the wicked, as
soon as they are loosened by death from the ruinous
habitation of their bodies, presently appear before
God, are condemned to hell, and are dragged by the
devil, hell's jailer, into that prison where they are
bound in chains of darkness, filled with horror and
anguish until the day of eternal judgment. The
Scripture tells us of disobedient spirits thrown into
prison (1 Peter 3:19–20).

Second, the wrath of God will come in fully upon
all the wicked together at the last day, called "the
day of judgment" and "the perdition of the ungodly"
(2 Peter 3:7). When the Lord Jesus shall come to
judge the world, He will bring the treasures of God's
wrath with Him and render unto all the wicked that
wrath and vengeance which is their due. Therefore
this day is called "the day of wrath and revelation of
the righteous judgment of God" (Romans 2:5). This
will be a dreadful day unto the wicked, when the
heavens shall pass away with a great noise and, like a
scroll, be rolled together; the elements shall melt
with fervent heat and be dissolved. It shall be a day
when the sun shall become black as sackcloth, and
the moon become like blood; when the powers of
heaven shall be shaken and the stars shall fall from
heaven to the earth like figs from a tree when it is
shaken with a mighty wind; when there shall be
thunderings exceedingly loud, and lightnings and

tempests exceedingly horrid; when the last trumpet shall sound and a mighty shout shall come down from above and awaken all the sinners who are asleep in the dust; when Christ the great Judge of the world shall come forth from His Father's house and make His appearance in the world with millions of mighty angels, and all the saints at His right hand clothed with majesty and brightness of glory; when the wicked shall come forth from their graves. As soon as they shall open their eyes they shall see heaven and earth on fire about their ears, and the Lord Jesus coming towards them in flaming fire to take vengeance upon them; as soon as they open their ears they shall hear the dreadful trumpet and shout in the air, and the howling and lamentations of all their fellow sinners about them upon the earth.

Oh, the dread and confusion which the wicked then shall be filled with when they are summoned and dragged to the tribunal seat of Christ, and there have the books opened before them where all their sins are written, and which will then be made manifest to the whole world; and when the sentence "Depart, ye cursed, into everlasting fire" shall be passed upon them; and when the Lord shall open the treasures of wrath to them, and give them that portion thereof which is their due; and when they shall see the mouth of hell open beneath them, and a horrible flame issuing forth from there, giving notice of a more horrible fire within which is prepared for them—oh, the dread! Oh, the shrieks! Who can dwell with such devouring fire! Who can inhabit such everlasting burnings! How welcome would a great rock or mountain be if they could find any that would fall upon them, and hide them from the wrath of the Lamb, and keep off the strokes of God's vengeance, which then will be inflicted upon them!

But, the sentence being pronounced, the execution will follow, and none can escape it. From Christ's tribunal seat, the wicked will be thrown into the fiery prison of hell, where they will be shut down and shut in, and that forever. There they will lie; there they will fry, and there they will cry; though always dying, they will never die. The fire there will burn most dreadfully and continually, and will never be extinguished. The wicked will be tormented there in every part and in extreme measure, and their torment will never be ended.

5. Who this Jesus is who delivers from wrath to come.

In the text He is called "Jesus," and the reason for this name we find in Matthew 1:21: "Thou shalt call His name Jesus, for He shall save His people from their sins." This Jesus is God and man in one person. He is the eternal Son of God, of the same essence with the Father, equal to Him in power and glory, who before the world was appointed in time to be the Redeemer of mankind; and when the fullness of time had come, He took upon Himself a true, human body and soul. He was conceived by the Holy Ghost, was born of a lowly virgin, lived in a lowly condition, was owned by a voice from heaven to be the only begotten and beloved Son of God. He preached the glad tidings of salvation to sinners, confirmed His doctrine by many miracles, died for the salvation of sinners (that being the cursed death of the cross), was raised up the third day, appeared to His disciples after His resurrection, and, after forty days, in the sight of many, ascended up to heaven where now He is at the right hand of God, making intercession for us.

6. How Jesus delivers from the wrath of God to come.

First, by His death, whereby He has purchased deliverance, having hereby satisfied God's justice. In His death, and in our place, Jesus underwent that punishment which our sins deserved. His body was nailed to the cross, which was an accursed death, and His soul was afflicted with the immediate impressions of God's wrath, which was so weighty and grievous that any mere creature would have sunk under it. But He, being God and man, bore up and broke through and got loose from the bands of death. The dignity of His person put a merit on His sufferings, especially the eternal compact or agreement between Him and His Father being such, and so became a sufficient satisfaction to justice, and that was accepted as fully as if sinners had done it in their own persons. We read that Jesus Himself "bore our sins in His body on the tree" (1 Peter 2:24); that "He gave His life a ransom for many" (Matthew 20:28); that we are "redeemed with His blood" (1 Peter 1:18–19); that we are "reconciled through His death" (Romans 5:10). Jesus delivers from wrath by His death, having therein undergone it Himself in place of His people.

Second, by His intercession, Christ delivers from wrath to come. Having offered up Himself as a sacrifice to satisfy divine justice for sin, He pleads the

merit of it at the right hand of God on behalf of
sinners for their redemption. He is called not only
our Surety, to satisfy for us (Hebrews 7:22), but also
our Advocate, to plead for us (1 John 2:1). Our deliverance from wrath to come, the damnation and
punishment of hell, proceeds not only from Christ's
death, whereby He has purchased it, but also from
His intercession, whereby He effectually accom-
plishes and obtains it. And therefore the apostle
joins both together in the procurement of freedom
from condemnation. Romans 8:34: "Who is he that
condemneth? It is Christ that died, yea, rather, is
risen again, who is even at the right hand of God,
who also maketh intercession for us." And upon this
account He is said to be able to save unto the uttermost. Hebrews 7:25: "Wherefore He is able to save
them to the uttermost, that do come unto God by
Him, seeing He ever liveth to make intercession for
them."

Third, by His mission, or sending His Spirit to
effectually call people to Himself, Jesus brings them
into a state of salvation, and gives them an actual interest in this deliverance, which He has purchased
for them. This leads to the next particular.

*7. How any do or may have a share in this deliverance by
Jesus from the wrath to come.*
This is by faith in Jesus Christ, which is wrought
by His Spirit in effectual calling. It occurs when the
Lord, by His Spirit, opens the eyes of sinners, con-
vinces them of the guilt and evil of their sins, awak-
ens their consciences, and works contrition and a
sense of their misery and danger; and when the

Lord shows and persuades them how utterly unable
they are to save themselves, that no reformation or
righteousness of their own, which either they have
or can attain unto, can procure deliverance from
wrath for them and, withal, that no mere creature in
the world is able to help in this case; and when the
Lord by His Spirit reveals Himself as the only Savior
and all-sufficient one, who is most willing to save
and deliver them, and withal most powerfully and
irresistibly and yet most sweetly bows their wills, and
inclines them to choose Him for their Savior, and,
grieving for sin and renouncing their own righteousness, to rest themselves upon Him for salvation. And this, accompanied with a free and resolved
delivering up of themselves to His teaching and
government, is effectual calling.

Herein the Lord, by His Spirit, draws and lays
hold on sinners, and enables them by faith to lay
hold on Him, and hence arises their union to Christ
and interest in Christ. And they come to have a
share in the deliverance by Christ from wrath to
come.

When the jailer cried out with trembling to Paul
and Silas, "Sirs, what must I do to be saved?" the direction given him was, "Believe on the Lord Jesus
Christ, and thou shalt be saved" (Acts 16:30–31). It is
faith that gives an interest in Christ, and hereby an
interest in the deliverance which He has purchased.
It is faith that unites us to Christ, whereby we are
said to be in Him, and there is no condemnation to
those who are in Christ Jesus (Romans 8:1). We are
justified by faith (Romans 5:1), and so are absolved
from the guilt of sin and all obligation to punish-

ment. The Lord Jesus Christ, having fully satisfied God's justice for our sins by His death in our place, and this being imputed to us through faith, and accounted as if we had done it ourselves (as a surety's paying our debt is accounted by the creditor as if we had paid it), we are acquitted, and no more exposed to the wrath of God and punishment of hell than if we had never committed any one sin to deserve it.

USE OF INFORMATION

1. See here the worth of Jesus. He is the Deliverer, and the only Deliverer from wrath to come. Jesus Christ is a person of the greatest worth in Himself; the divine and human natures, being united in Him, render Him infinitely glorious and altogether lovely. And hence it is that He is replenished with such transcendent excellencies and perfections as are not to be found again in any creature, either in earth or heaven. Jesus Christ is esteemed to be the most worthy person by those who know Him and understand what real worth is, especially sinners, when awakened, and made sensible of the curse which lies upon them for sin, and the wrath of God which hangs over them. And when they come to apprehend how fearful a thing it is to fall under the strokes of God's vengeance, and see no way of escape but by Jesus, the only Deliverer from future wrath, then, of all persons and things in the world, Jesus Christ is most precious to them. Never did there appear in the world a person of such high dignity, of such admirable beauty and such wonderful love as the Lord Jesus Christ, who came down from the Father and clothed Himself with our na-

ture that He might become our Savior, Redeemer, Surety, and Advocate, and that He might deliver us from wrath to come.

2. See here the value of Christ's death. Hebrews 9:22: "Without shedding of blood, there is no remission of sin." And if there is no remission, then there is no deliverance from wrath to come; if guilt remains, punishment will ensue, and that of God's eternal wrath in hell. It was not the blood of bulls and goats sacrificed under the law that could remove guilt and procure remission of sin. Hebrews 10:4: "For it is not possible that the blood of bulls and goats should take away sin." But it was through Christ's sacrifice of Himself once for all, and shedding His blood upon the cross, that remission of sins and, by consequence, this deliverance from wrath to come were purchased. It was not thousands of rams, or ten thousand rivers of oil, or all the treasures of the earth that could have procured remission of sin, because all this would have been no satisfaction unto God's justice; but the blood of Jesus, who is God–man, has satisfied God's justice. By His death, Christ has paid the full price which was due for sin. Surely, then, His death is of greater value than the riches of ten thousand worlds, were there that many.

3. Here see the excellency of faith. We read in Peter's first epistle of a precious Christ (2:7), and of Christ's precious blood (1:19), and also of precious faith (1:7). Of all other graces, faith is called precious, and it has above other graces a peculiar excellence; not so much in respect to itself, but in regard to its object, as it gives interest in the precious

Christ and makes application of His precious blood. By this, we come to attain a share in this deliverance by Christ from wrath to come. Christ is most precious as the Author of our deliverance; Christ's death is most precious as the merit of our deliverance; and faith is most precious as the instrument of our deliverance.

4. Here see what a privilege it is to have the gospel preached among us. The gospel is a means to make discovery unto us of Jesus Christ, the only Deliverer from wrath to come, and also a means to work faith in us, which comes by hearing (Romans 10:17). Hereby alone we come to have interest in Jesus Christ and His deliverance. Such as are without the gospel are in darkness and unbelief, and are hastening forward towards the regions of eternal darkness; and they do not know where they are going. It is of more use to have the light of the gospel than to have the light of the sun; and the total removal of this light is a greater judgment than any temporal calamity, since it is the means to prevent eternal misery.

USE OF EXAMINATION

Is Jesus the only Deliverer from wrath to come? It concerns all of you, then, to examine yourselves as to whether you have an interest in this Jesus, and the deliverance from wrath which He has purchased, and which is through Him alone to be obtained. All of you are sinners. You were born in sin, you have lived in sin, and, should you die in sin, as certainly as the guilt of sin lies upon you, so certainly will the wrath of God come upon you. Without an interest in

Jesus Christ, there can be no escaping for you. You
may know whether you have an interest in Jesus
Christ by your faith, by your life, by your love, by your
likeness, and by your obedience.

1. If you have an interest in Jesus Christ, then you
have faith. I don't mean a historical faith, only believing the history and report which the gospel gives
of Jesus Christ, what He has done and suffered. Nor
do I mean a temporary faith, which is the fond pre-
sumption of some formal hypocrites, whereby they
may seem to cleave unto Christ when, indeed, their
hearts cleave chiefly to sin; whereby, through mis-
apprehension of gospel privileges, and misapplica-
tion of gospel promises, they may attain to some
kind of fleshly love and joy, which endures but a
while (it usually ends in open apostasy). But if you
have a true interest in Christ, you have a true, justifying faith whereby, being first convinced of sin,
humbled and emptied of yourselves, resolvedly part-
ing with all your sins as to affection, and sincerely
renouncing all your own righteousness as to depen-
dence, you cast yourselves upon Christ, lean and de-
pend upon Him, expecting remission and salvation
only through His perfect righteousness made yours
by imputation.

Have you, by faith, discerned Christ? Have you, by
faith, applied Christ? Are you, by faith, joined to
Christ? Have you been, by faith, taken off your own
foundations, and built upon Christ the chief
Cornerstone? Have you, by faith, been cut off from
your old stock, and engrafted into Christ the choice
Vine? Have you, by faith, been divorced from sin and
married unto Christ, the best Husband? Have you

gotten unto and into Christ by faith? And have you received Him into your hearts by faith? Without this true faith, there can be union to Christ; without union to Christ, there can be no interest in Christ; without interest in Christ, there can be no remission of sin, no salvation and deliverance from wrath to come.

2. If you have an interest in Christ, you have life. 1 John 5:12: "He that hath the Son hath life, and he that hath not the Son hath not life." He who has an interest in Christ, the Son of God, has life. He shall have eternal life hereafter, and he has spiritual life, which is eternal life begun here. These, besides the natural life which they received from the parents in their generation, have a principle of spiritual life, which they receive from the Spirit of God in their regeneration. They are the only persons who are quickened from their spiritual death; but he who does not have the Son does not have life. Such shall never see life hereafter, but the wrath of God abides on them (John 3:36). Plus, they are spiritually dead here, dead in trespasses and sins (Ephesians 2:1).

You may know whether you have an interest in Jesus Christ by your spiritual life. I do not say by your constant liveliness, for this may be wanting at some times in true believers, but you may know it by your spiritual life. You were dead, but now you are alive; and you may know your spiritual life by your spiritual motion from sin and towards God; by your spiritual senses to discern between good and evil; by your spiritual appetite after Christ and His righteousness, and communion with God in His ordinances and the like. If these are not symptoms of this spiritual life in you, it is a sign that Christ is not in you; you have no interest in Him and His deliverance.

3. If you have an interest in Christ, you have love. You love Christ in sincerity (Ephesians 6:24: "Grace be with all them that love our Lord Jesus in sincerity") and you love Christ supremely (Matthew 10:37: "He that loveth father or mother more than Me is not worthy of Me"). If any man or woman loves any person or thing in the world more than Jesus Christ, they are unworthy of Him and have no interest in Him or any of His benefits. And therefore a dreadful curse is pronounced upon such as do not love Christ. 1 Corinthians 16:22: "If any man love not the Lord Jesus Christ, let him be Anathema Maranatha." That is, let him be cursed until the Lord comes; and when the Lord comes the wrath of God will also come upon him.

4. If you have an interest in Christ, you have likeness. You are like unto Christ; you have His image upon you. Jesus Christ is formed in you (Galatians 4:19). You are like Christ in your disposition, in humility, meekness, heavenliness, and the like. You are not perfectly like Him, yet in some measure you are. And you imitate Him more and more, and endeavor after more conformity to His image. Where pride reigns instead of humility, where inordinate anger reigns instead of meekness, where malice and revenge reign instead of love and forgiveness, where the love of the world reigns instead of heavenly-mindedness, where evil concupiscence reigns instead of mortified affections, such are without likeness to Christ and without interest in Christ. Those who are graceless are also Christless, and cannot

escape future wrath.

5. If you have an interest in Christ, you have obedience. Your faith shows itself in your works (James 2:18). And your love shows itself in your keeping Christ's commands (John 14:21). Such as do not obey Christ's laws, but cast His commandments behind their backs, and will not have this Lord to rule over them, have neither faith, nor love, nor life, nor likeness unto Christ; and therefore be sure that they have no interest in Him.

Test your interest in Christ, the only Deliverer from future wrath, by these marks.

USE OF REPROOF AND TERROR

If upon search you find you are without an interest in Christ, allow this word of reproof. Sinners, what do you think? Is there no such thing as wrath to come? Is there no such place as hell, where the damned shall be eternally tormented? What blackmouth is there who dares to speak against this truth which is so clearly revealed in the Word of God? Surely none but such as are children of the devil; the father of lies will impeach the Word of God with falsehood, and hereby make God a liar, who has foretold this so plainly in Scripture. Only such as are loose in their lives and deficient in their morals, whose interest they think it is to do so, will deny the punishment by eternal fire in hell so that they might sin with fewer checks and controls. But when they come to feel the heat of this fire, as of all others they are most likely to be cast into everlasting burnings, then they will be of another mind.

And if there is such dreadful wrath coming, such

a horrible fire being prepared in hell for all disobedient persons, for all impenitent persons, for all
hypocrites and unbelievers, what do you so, sinners?
Have you not sinned? Have you not by your sins deserved hell's burnings? And are you not by your sins
exposed unto the vengeance of eternal fire? Is there
any way for you to escape but by Jesus Christ, the
only Deliverer from wrath to come? And do you yet
neglect Him? Do you refuse and reject Him? Do you
shut the door of your hearts against Him? What! Do
you think only of what your bodies shall eat, what
you shall drink, and wherewith you shall be clothed?
Do you think only of providing for a short abode in
this world, and in the meantime neglect your salvation of your souls, and take no care to prevent your
everlasting punishment? Are you not guilty of a
greater affront and indignity against God, when He
has made such provision for your salvation as to
send His Son into the world for you, and to offer His
Son with deliverance to you? Don't you sin against
the greatest expression of His love to mankind?
Don't you spurn Him, and in effect say, "God might
have kept His Son to Himself for all I care!" Are you
not guilty of the greatest ingratitude towards the
Lord Jesus Christ?

Never was there such a thing heard of since the
foundation of the world; never could such a thing
have entered into your thoughts or desires as the
Lord Jesus has freely, and of His own accord, done
for you. It is a most stupendous thing which, I think,
should fill you with astonishment and admiration:
that the Lord of glory should take your flesh, make
Himself of no reputation, and humble Himself unto

death, even the cursed death of the cross, and all so that He might deliver you from the curse of the law, the wrath to come and the pains of hell forever. Now, when Christ, by His death, has fully satisfied God's justice for your sins, and purchased eternal life for your souls, and out of wonderful kindness has caused the everlasting gospel and glad tidings of salvation to be made known in this little nook of the earth, and cast your lot in such a spot of ground as the like is not to be found again under the whole scope of heaven for the pure and powerful preaching of the gospel; I say, when Jesus Christ has sent His faithful ministers to you (whom you may find and hear if you will look after them) with this message, to tell you what Christ has done for you, and to make tenders of Him with all His benefits to you; when Christ lets you know how able and willing He is to save you, and knocks at the door of your hearts for entertainment—if though you are such helpless and miserable creatures without Him, you should, notwithstanding all this, refuse or neglect Christ, prefer some base lust before Him, and serve the devil rather than be saved by Christ, hereby you express great contempt of Christ and are guilty of horrid ingratitude. Hereby you trample His blood under your feet, and in effect you say that He might have spared His pains in coming down from heaven, that He might have stayed until He had been sent for, that He might have carried His gospel to any other place, for all you value it or Him.

Thus you deal with Christ and thrust Him away from you, though He comes upon the most welcome errand, and ought to be received with all readiness and thankfulness. And think, sinner, moreover how injurious you are hereby unto yourselves, what folly and madness you are guilty of. Do you know what you are? If you do, you know that without Christ you are cursed wretches and children of wrath.

Behold this wonder in Christ: everlasting burnings have become everlasting mercies. And he who will come at the last day as a Judge in flaming fire to take vengeance upon you, if you are found without an interest in Him, now offers to be your Savior and Advocate to deliver you from the wrath to come. And is it not the height of folly and sottishness to slight and refuse such a person, and, by refusing Him, to plunge yourselves into unavoidable ruin and destruction?

When you may have Christ, and with Him all things needful in this world, and that with greater security than by all your inordinate desires and endeavors, and moreover such riches as exceed all earthly treasures, and besides this a crown of glory in the other world; when, notwithstanding this, you choose to neglect Christ and choose rather the pleasures of sin for a season, the gratifying of some base lusts unto the everlasting damnation of your souls and bodies in hell; to refuse, with Christ, everlasting happiness, and headlong to run yourselves into everlasting burnings—if this is not folly and madness, I don't know what is!

You can't contrive or cause greater mischief and injury to yourselves; for I am persuaded that such as go to hell out of England, especially out of London, where they have or might have such plentiful means of grace, of all others will have the lowest and hottest place. Oh, how it will sting and gnaw, rack and torture you forever to remember what seasons and opportunities, what calls and invitations you had; but by your neglect of getting an interest in the Lord Jesus, the Deliverer from wrath to come, you have brought ruin upon yourselves. Think, sinners, how unavoidable the wrath to come is without an interest in Christ; and think, oh, think how intolerable this wrath will be when it has come! "Who can dwell with devouring fire?" Think of the extremity of pain and anguish which is prepared for you; think of the eternity of hell's torments, that when you have been there as many thousands and millions of years as there are stars or sands, your torment will be but beginning. Never, never, never will it have any ending. I think this should terrify all Christless sinners who are already condemned to this place of torment. John 3:18: "He that believeth not is condemned already." And you do not know how soon execution may follow the sentence. If you die this night out of Christ, the wrath of God will seize upon you immediately, and you will be irrecoverably miserable, and that to eternity.

USE OF COMFORT

This comfort is for all those who, upon trial, find well-grounded evidence of their interest in this Jesus, the only Deliverer from wrath to come. You are the only persons in the world who are in a safe condition (Romans 8:33–34). Who shall lay anything to your charge? If God does not charge you with guilt, who can charge you besides? Through Christ, God justifies you. He pardons all your sins as if they

had never been committed, and accepts you as perfectly righteous through the perfect righteousness
of Christ, which has been made yours by faith. Who
is it who can condemn you? The law may condemn
you, conscience may condemn you; but since Christ
died for you, and in His death was condemned and
suffered in your place, you are freed from the condemnation of God and the eternal damnation of
hell.

Now, being out of all danger of future wrath, you
may the better bear any evil of affliction which in
this world may be your portion. You may now com-
fortably wait for the coming of Christ from heaven,
whom God has raised from the dead, even this Jesus
who has delivered you from wrath to come, and who
will bring for you, and give to you, everlasting glory
and happiness at the day of His second appearance.

USE OF EXHORTATION

Let this exhort such as are without an interest in
Christ, the Deliverer from wrath to come. Oh, be
persuaded, without any further delay, to flee from
this wrath of God, which pursues you and will overtake you ere long; this is done by fleeing unto, and
getting an interest in, this Jesus, who alone can deliver you. Oh, that I might be instrumental in bringing some of you to close with Jesus Christ! Sinners,
will you be persuaded at length to accept Christ? You
may have Him, and you must have Him; otherwise
you are cursed, you are lost, and you cannot escape
eternal death and wrath. If you would be delivered
from wrath to come by Jesus Christ, take these few
directions:

1. Labor for a thorough sense of your absolute
need of Christ, and that not only by reason of your
guilt of sin and danger of hell, but also that there is
no salvation or deliverance attainable by any other
way but by Jesus Christ. Do not think that your repentance and reformation, though these are necessary, and without which there can be no salvation
for you, can save you without Christ. If you should attain these, and rest in these, you will as certainly go
to hell as the most wicked transgressor. You cannot
be saved by any of your own righteousness, because
your righteousness is imperfect, and therefore cannot satisfy God's justice for your sins, and therefore
cannot deliver you from wrath to come. Should you
weep for your sins till your eyes were cried out, and
sigh and grieve for sin till your hearts were broken;
should you wear your knees to the bone with kneel-
ing, wear your tongues to the roots with praying,
and consume your flesh to nothing with fasting;
should you be as just, temperate, charitable, and as
strictly religious as anyone breathing, yea, as holy
for the future as any angel in heaven, all this would
not wipe away the guilt of your sin or deliver you out
of the hands of God's justice, which must be satisfied.

One has said very well that if any would be saved
by their own righteousness, they must first go to
hell, and there continue in torments to eternity; and
if that could be supposed which cannot be supposed
to be done—because there is no ending of those
torments which are eternal, and therefore there is
no possibility of getting loose from them—yet, sup-
posing that anyone could do this, they must come

back and fulfill the law in every tittle. Both of these being impossible for you who are guilty of sin, you have absolute need of Christ's perfect righteousness in order to be delivered from wrath to come.

It is this which damns and sinks many thousands in hell: looking and seeking to be saved by a righteousness of their own. I know that most are damned for their unrighteousness, and go to hell in the broader way of gross impiety and wickedness; yet if that is the broader way and has its ten thousands, this too is broad and has its thousands. Besides the more sober among the heathens, who believed in a future state of happiness and looked to arrive at it by moral righteousness; besides the papists, who assert justification by their works, and that we are no otherwise justified than as we are made internally righteous, and this expressing itself in acts of obedience; besides Socinians and other sects, together with the Quakers, who plainly affirm that we must be saved by a righteousness within, which the Quakers call "Christ within" (all of whom fundamentally err in their judgments concerning the righteousness which alone can save—besides these, it is natural to all to seek salvation this way.

All are born under a covenant of works; they are under the law and not under grace, and when any think how they shall be saved, they immediately set to work and seek a righteousness of their own. They seek to fulfill the law themselves, and hope that if they repent and lead a new life, though they have sinned, God will be merciful, and will pardon and save them.

It is an ordinary thing that, even where the light

of truth most clearly shines and the gospel is most powerfully preached, when any are convinced of sin by the beams of this light, and awakened out of their security by some powerful sermon that reveals their danger of eternal ruin as the just desert of sin, they will cry out with the Philppian jailer, "What shall we do to be saved?" And however they are directed, as he was, to believe, yet most rest in doing, not believing.

They fall immediately upon confession of sin and sorrowing for it; they fall upon reforming. They will not be drunk or swear, commit adultery or break the Sabbath, or defraud in their dealings. They now begin to hear the Word, to pray with their families and in secret, to keep days of fasting, and conform unto all these external acts of devotion. And if they can attain to some kind of flashy affection, they think all is well. If they find their hearts dull, cold, and hard, they may also be troubled for it—not upon a right gospel account, but because they feel they lack such a righteousness to present God with as they desire, or through some secret fear that their righteousness will not hold water. But all this while these persons seek after salvation through a self-righteousness, and Christ is left out. His righteousness is either unknown or utterly disregarded and neglected by them. And thus many go to hell in a way of duty. Their duties are the occasion of their damnation through their resting in them.

It may seem strange that any should have hopes of salvation by imperfect service, but this, I suppose, may come to pass either because they don't mind the imperfections of their services (for lack of understanding the law in its spirituality, and examining themselves by it), or through misapprehensions that God's mercy revealed in His Word will pardon them. They do not consider that all His special mercy in pardoning and saving is through Christ; nor do they consider that God is infinitely just and righteous as well as merciful, and that there is no room for the exercise of mercy towards sinners until justice is satisfied; they do not consider that God's justice requires a perfect righteousness, otherwise there cannot be a perfect justification; they do not consider that there must be full satisfaction of God's justice for the breach of God's law, otherwise there can be no clear remission, and that there must be perfect righteousness made out some way, or else we cannot be accepted by God as righteous.

Since, therefore, this satisfaction of God's justice cannot be made by ourselves, because, being finite, we cannot make an infinite compensation which infinite justice requires; and since perfect righteousness, which must include both original and actual, cannot be in us who are guilty both of original and actual sin; and since the least sin renders forever a personal, perfect righteousness impossible; and since the law curses everyone who does not continue in all things which are written in the book of the law to do them; therefore, as many as are of the law, who seek justification by the way of works or the righteousness of the law, are under the curse (Galatians 3:10). It is clear that whoever expects to be saved from wrath to come cannot do so by their own righteousness, but by another's righteousness, namely the righteousness of Christ. If you would attain an interest in Christ, you must be sensible of your need of Him and His righteousness upon this account.

2. Labor for a thorough acquaintance with the nature, intention, and efficacy of the righteousness of Christ. The apostle said of the Jews, in Romans 10:2–4, "I bear them record that they have a zeal of God, but not according to knowledge. For they, being ignorant of God's righteousness, and going about to establish their own righteousness, have not submitted themselves to the righteousness of God. For Christ is the end of the law for righteousness unto everyone that believeth." And as it was with the Jews of old, so it is with many nominal Christians now, who may be led only by a blind zeal to work out their own salvation in a way of doing. This is through their ignorance of the righteousness of Christ, called here in Romans "the righteousness of God," either because it is the only righteousness which God will accept, or because it is the righteousness which God has provided for men, which sense it must have. Romans 3:21–22: "But now the righteousness of God without the law is manifest, even the righteousness of God, which is by faith in Jesus Christ." This is the righteousness which God accepts and has appointed for our justification.

Or else it is called the righteousness of God because it is the righteousness of Christ, who is God-man, no other righteousness than of such a person being sufficient for man in his fallen state. Through the ignorance of this righteousness of Christ, many Christians seeking after righteousness go about to establish their own righteousness (that is, a personal righteousness), endeavor the gaining of

heaven in a way of doing, and do not submit themselves to the righteousness of God. It is through
pride (so natural to everyone) that they are loath to
be beholden wholly unto another. They would have
something of their own to commend them to God;
and therefore they do not submit unto the
righteousness of Christ which God has provided for
them.

Therefore you must labor to be clear in your understanding of what this righteousness of Christ is.
There are two things required of and absolutely
necessary to fallen man. The first is satisfaction
unto God's justice for his sins. Without this there
can be no escape from eternal death and misery, because guilt obliges unto punishment, and this cannot be removed until God's justice is satisfied. The
other is perfect, actual obedience to God's law.
Without this there can be no attaining eternal life
and glory. The first covenant of works, given to man
in his fallen state, would still be in force: "Do this
and live," and "the soul that sinneth shall die." Now
man, being finite, cannot satisfy God's justice for
his sins. And, being a sinner, he cannot yield perfect, actual obedience to God's law. But the Lord
Jesus Christ has done both for man.

By His suffering and death upon the cross, Christ
made satisfaction of God's justice, being made a
curse for us (Galatians 3:13). And under-going
equivalent punishment, punishment unto the
damned's torments, and being God-man, though
only the human nature suffered, yet the divine
nature in the same person put an infinite value
upon the sufferings of the human nature, and so

became a sufficient satisfaction of God's infinite justice. And hereby He has purchased redemption of sins and deliverance from wrath to come.

Christ has yielded a perfect, actual obedience unto the law. He has fulfilled all righteousness so that, not having a perfect righteousness of our own, His might be made ours, and we might attain life thereby. This passive and active obedience is the righteousness of Christ, which you should labor to understand. Also understand that Christ did not have this righteousness for Himself. He had no sin of His own for which to suffer; but it was in our place and as our Surety. This righteousness was intended for us, and, being the righteousness of such a person, is highly efficacious to attain that for which it was designed, as will appear by the covenant.

3. Labor for a thorough understanding of the covenant, both the covenant which God made with Christ on behalf of man and the covenant which God has made with man through Christ.

Acquaint yourselves with the covenant God made with Christ on behalf of man. Whatever worth and value there was in the righteousness of Christ, yet God might have required a personal righteousness and satisfaction, and Christ's righteousness might have stood us in no stead. But God eternally covenanted and agreed with Christ that if He would take human nature, and work out a righteousness for fallen man, it would be accepted; that if He would take to Himself the body of a man that God would prepare for Him, and make His soul an offering for sin, that is, suffer what His justice required for the sins of man, He would see His seed and justify many (Isaiah 53:10–11). It is through this covenant with Christ that Christ's righteousness is accepted on behalf of sinners, God having agreed before that it should so be.

Acquaint yourselves with the covenant which God has made with man through Christ, where upon the account of Christ God has promised remission of sins and eternal life. Hebrews 10:16–17: "This is My covenant that I will make with them, saith the Lord: I will put My laws into their hearts, and their sins and iniquities I will remember no more."

1 John 2:25: "This is the promise which He hath promised, even eternal life." If ever you are saved from eternal wrath and attain eternal life, it must be by virtue of this new covenant of grace, wherein God engages to give what His Son has purchased.

Labor to be acquainted with the nature and use of faith, which is the tenor of the covenant of grace. The tenor of the covenant of works was "Do this and live." The tenor of, or that which is required to have an interest in, the covenant of grace is "Believe and live." Faith joins the soul unto Christ, the Mediator of this covenant, and gives an actual interest in Him and His purchase, as well as whatever is promised through Him in the covenant. Faith is the soul resting alone on Christ, and applying the promises of pardon and life unto the soul. Faith is not only a discerning, but applying or laying hold of Christ's righteousness outside us, whereby it is imputed to us or accounted as ours by God, as if it had been our own personal righteousness. If ever you would be justified, that is, have your sins pardoned and your persons accepted as perfectly righteous in the sight of God, it must be by faith. You must renounce your own righteousness as imperfect and insufficient, apprehending and applying, resting and trusting in Christ's perfect righteousness.

4. Apply yourselves unto God in prayer, that He, having given His Son for you, would also give Him to you, and that He would give you faith to receive and apply Him. Beg this again and again, with confession of your sins and the sense of your want of Christ; never stop asking until you obtain. Also attend upon the Word where it is preached most purely and powerfully for the working of faith, which comes by hearing (Romans 10:17). And then, in the strength of the Lord, put forth your hand to lay hold of Christ, and labor to cast yourselves upon Him, resigning withal yourselves up to Him not only to be saved, but also to be taught and ruled by Him.

OBJECTION. I know someone will object, "If we seek thus to be delivered from wrath to come by Jesus Christ, and by faith in His righteousness outside us, and not by internal righteousness or that of works, this will open a door to licentiousness."

ANSWER. This is an old objection against the doctrine of justification by faith, even in the days of the Apostles, when the doctrine was first preached. But, as then, so also now, this doctrine does not give any liberty to sin; for however we cannot be saved *by* inherent righteousness and any of our good works, yet we cannot be saved *without* them. None can assert more highly that there must be regeneration and sanctification, a new heart and a new life; otherwise

there can be no admission into heaven and no escaping the damnation of hell.

Yea, further, we say that the same faith which is
an instrument of justification is also a part of sanctification, being a heart-purifying grace (Acts 15:9). As
faith is a hand to lay hold of Christ's righteousness,
so it is a hand to receive supplies of grace and spirit
from Christ to quicken us unto newness of life. Yea,
I may say, there can be no real, inherent righteousness without an interest by faith in Christ's imputed
righteousness. There may be a righteousness of
some kind like it, but not of the right kind, not a
righteousness which springs from the true principle
of faith, and therefore it cannot be a righteousness
that is pleasing to God; for "without faith it is impossible to please God" (Hebrews 11:6).

So if you would have inherent righteousness, and
walk so as to please God, you must believe on the
Lord Jesus, and fetch grace from Him in whom all
the fullness of Deity dwells (Colossians 1:19). If you
would have lust mortified, the world crucified, and
overcome the devil, who endeavors by his temptations to draw you unto sin, you must draw virtue and
strength to do it by faith. In a word, if you would
deny ungodliness and worldly lusts, and live soberly,
righteously, and godly in this present evil world, you
must do it by faith. But how to attain the principle
and practice of godliness, I will address in the last
part of this book.

Had I room, I might speak much by way of exhortation to such as have attained an interest in Christ
and the deliverance purchased by Him. In a word,
learn to admire free grace, to be very thankful and

watchful, to endeavor to bring others to Christ, to adorn your profession, to be blameless and harmless, the disciples of Christ without rebuke in the midst of a crooked and perverse generation, among whom you should shine as lights in the world here, so that you may shine like stars, yea, like suns in the kingdom of your Father forever.

Godliness in Principle and Conversation

a necessary preparative to the world's dissolution
and the escaping of future burnings

"Seeing then that all these things shall be dissolved,
what manner of persons ought ye to be in all holy
conversation and godliness?" 2 Peter 3:11

T he Apostle Peter, who was one of Christ's
twelve disciples, foreseeing His second coming, says that in the latter days scoffers will
arise, whom he describes to be persons "walking after their own lusts," who would mock at the predic-
tion and promise thereof. They will say, "Where is
the promise of His coming? For since the fathers
fell asleep, all things continue as they were from the
beginning of the creation."

And surely, if any age has produced such scoffers,
it is this age, wherein so many lewd and lustful persons abound, who are debauched in their morals
and endeavor to debauch themselves and others in
their intellectual pursuits. They are profane and vicious in their practices, endeavoring to throw off all
Christian principles. They give themselves up to the
service of the devil and their own lusts, to work all
uncleanness and wickedness with greediness that
they may have no feeling or sense of their danger,
that they may sin without any remorse and trouble

of conscience. They endeavor to work themselves
into a persuasion that the coming of the Lord Jesus
to judge the world is a mere fable. They see that one
generation goes and another comes, and they persuade themselves that it was so always without any
sign of the world's dissolution. From this they conclude that it will still continue, and that either this
world shall never have an end, or, at least, when
their life is at an end there shall then be a total end
of them; that there will be no resurrection; that
there will be no account for them to appear before
Christ's tribunal seat to be judged and to receive the
punishment which they have deserved for their sins.

In response to this, the Apostle:

1. Enervates and overthrows the plea of scoffers
from the world's continuance as it is from the beginning of the creation by putting them in mind of
that which they are willingly ignorant of, namely
the overthrow of the ungodly world of old by the
flood (2 Peter 3:5–6).

2. He gives us to understand that as certainly as
the old world was drowned with water, so certainly
the heavens and earth that now exist are reserved in
store, and shall be burned with fire at the last day in
the judgment and perdition of the ungodly (verse 7).

3. He shows that however the time between the
promise of Christ's second coming and the fulfilling of it might seem long to us, who measure the
length of time according to our short continuance
in the world, unto whom our short and hasty days
seem to be the longer and more tedious because of
our many troubles and miseries, yet unto the Lord
the time is short, in whose sight a thousand years

are but as one day (verse 8).

4. He lets us know that the Lord is not slack to fulfill His promise, which in its time shall be accomplished, but the reason for His deferring His coming and long-suffering towards sinners is out of pity towards them that they might not perish; that now they might take some course to avoid their ruin, which at His appearance will be unavoidable; that by His goodness and forbearance they might be moved and led to repentance (verse 9).

5. The Apostle then sets forth the day of the Lord's second coming by the certainty of it, by the suddenness of it, and by the dreadfulness of it.

First, by the certainty of it: The day of the Lord will come. It is appointed; it is promised; and it shall certainly be accomplished.

Second, by the suddenness of it: It will be like a thief in the night. It will be at a time when there is not the least expectation of it.

Third, by the dreadfulness of it: "The heavens then shall pass away with a great noise, and the elements shall melt with fervent heat; the earth also and its works shall be burned up" (verse 10). And, oh, the horror of the wicked when heaven and earth shall be on fire about them, and the Lord Jesus shall come in a flaming fire to take vengeance upon them!

6. The use which the Apostle makes of this doctrine concerning the world's dissolution at the day of Christ's second appearance is in the text: "Seeing then that all these things shall be dissolved, what manner of persons ought ye to be in all holy conversation and godliness?"

DOCTRINE: All these things shall be dissolved.

USE: Seeing it is so, what manner of persons ought we to be in all holy conversation and godliness? The answer is included in these words: in all holy conversation and godliness. That is, we ought to be persons of godliness and a holy conversation. We ought to be persons of godliness in regard to the principle of it; and we ought to be persons of godliness in regard to the practice of it in a holy conversation.

Hence observe:

DOCTRINE: Godliness in principle and conversation is a necessary preparative unto the world's dissolution and the escaping of future burnings.

There is a day coming when time shall have its conclusion and the world shall have its dissolution; when time shall be no more, and the world shall be no more. So the end of time and the end of the world shall be together. As there was a first day, so there shall be a last day; and as certainly as the world was created by God's Word at first, so certainly shall it be destroyed by fire at last. I conceive that this dissolution of the world will be, though on the day of judgment, still after Christ has finished the judgment and sentenced all to their eternal state; when He has conveyed the righteous unto the palace and mansions prepared for them in heaven, where no flame of fire shall be able to enter, and the wicked are left behind upon the earth full of horror and trembling through the apprehensions of that everlasting fire and punishment to which they are unalterably judged. Then the Lord Jesus, in His passage with the saints and angels unto the heaven of

heavens, will set this visible world on fire, while all
the wicked men and women who ever lived are on it.

Revelation 20:11: "Before His face, heaven and
earth shall flee away and no more place be found for
them." When He has finished His judging work
upon the white throne, He shall look to heaven and
earth and give a word of command; they shall immediately be set on fire and melt, and dissolve into
nothing, as if they had never existed. Nothing will
remain but the heaven of heavens—which is removed above all visible heavens where Christ is now
in His glory, and where the saints shall eternally
partake of His glory—and hell, where devils and
damned spirits now are, and where the wicked shall
be eternally tormented.

It may be that this fire will begin in the visible
heaven. It is said that the heavens shall pass away
with a great noise. It will be a dreadful noise indeed,
which the fire in the heavens above will make when
all the huge and vast orbs shall burst asunder and
crack to pieces; when they shall, with this vehement
heat, be rolled together like a scroll and shriveled
into nothing; when all the great luminaries over our
heads, some of them bigger than the earth, shall be
on fire together, and so melt and consume away.
The unframing and dissolving of the great heavens
above by the fire will be with great noise and horror
unto the wicked below. This will be accompanied
with a dissolving also of the elements, setting the
whole earth on fire: cities, houses, woods, fields,
mountains, earth, and air will all be turned into fire.
The wicked, most likely, will be in the midst of these
flames until all is consumed but them; and then

they shall be conveyed unto the most horrible and unquenchable and eternal burnings of hell. What tongue can express this? What heart can conceive of the anguish and pain of the wicked and ungodly world at this last day of the world's dissolution and destruction by fire?

USE. "Seeing then all these things shall be dissolved, what manner of persons ought ye to be in all holy conversation and godliness?" None but such as are godly persons, and of a holy conversation, will escape these future burnings. Therefore, I shall press all of you who read this to endeavor to attain the principle of godliness, and to live in the practice of godliness, so that you may be counted worthy to escape those dreadful things which shall befall the wicked at the day of Christ's second appearance.

In a former discourse I showed that Jesus Christ is this Deliverer, and that it is through faith alone in His imputed righteousness that any share in this deliverance. Yet, lest any should pretend that they have faith, and presume that they shall have deliverance through Christ while they are unholy in their hearts and lives, I have added this present discourse on godliness in principle and conversation, which is an inseparable companion and perpetual consequence of true justifying and saving faith, without which faith is dead and will prove altogether ineffectual unto salvation. Therefore give me leave to exhort and press you to labor after this godliness.

1. Labor after a principle of godliness. Godliness is begun in regeneration and conversion. Be persuaded to get new hearts, to become new creatures. Be persuaded to labor as in Ephesians 4:22–24, "to

put off (as concerning your former conversation) the old man, which is corrupt according to deceitful lusts, that you may be renewed in the spirit of your mind, and put on the new man, which after God is created in righteousness and true holiness." It is this alone which will denominate you as being godly in truth. And here I shall, besides the motive of the text, spread before you other motives to quicken you, and give you some directions to guide and help you in your endeavors after godliness.

MOTIVE 1. Consider the excellency of godliness. Godliness, or a gracious principle, is a jewel, a jewel of great scarcity in the world; it is very rarely found. There are many men and women in the world, but few Christians; many Christians, but few professors; many professors, but few who are seriously and thoroughly godly. It is a jewel of great worth; above all jewels it most enriches and adorns. Godliness is a shining beam which comes down from the Father of lights, a small rivulet which issues forth from God, the fountain of goodness. It is the beauty and luster of the soul, the image of God in man, the divine nature. It is the new life of the soul, the first fruit of eternal happiness, the dawning and budding of everlasting glory.

None are as high-born as the godly who are new-born; such are the royal seed of heaven, the begotten of God Himself, the sons and daughters of the Lord Almighty (James 1:18; 2 Corinthians 6:18). Godly persons are really the most honorable, being so nearly related to the King of Glory. They are the most beautiful persons, being transformed into the image of Him who is altogether lovely, and whose beauty is infinite and transcendent. Godly persons (however mean in outward appearance, however despised and vilified by the blind world) have in truth the greatest worth, and none are as excellently qualified and accomplished as they. They are all glorious within; their souls have such robes and ornaments upon them as all the external glory with which Solomon was arrayed is not comparable thereunto.

Ungodliness degrades, deforms, defiles, and renders men more vile than beasts; yea, by it princes and noblemen become slaves and vassals to the devil. But godliness wipes off filth and deformity, and advances men and women to the highest dignity; though they are persons of the meanest extract in the world, they become nobles and princes belonging to the court of heaven. None are so highly esteemed by God, the King of heaven and earth as the godly. God does not esteem any for their wealth, honor, worldly dignity, parts, learning, and worldly wisdom—those things without godliness are set at nought by God—but godliness is of high account with Him, even in those who are very mean in all other regards. God honors the godly who honor Him, but the ungodly who dishonor Him are lightly esteemed by Him (1 Samuel 2:30).

The angels, those noble couriers of heaven, are attendants and ministering spirits unto us, which shows the esteem which they have for those who are godly (Hebrews 1:14). Yea, upon the earth, and also in the dark world, godliness casts forth some beams of brightness, which render it illustrious in the eyes of those who behold it; and that not only in the eyes of the righteous (who esteem godliness in others

and themselves too above all other attainments and
enjoyments, and who would rather part with liberty,
all that they have, and life itself rather than this
jewel), but also in the eyes of the wicked who,
though they have an enmity in their hearts against
godliness, yet they have an esteem in their mind and
judgment for it. Though they hate it, they reverence
it; and though they do not endeavor after it, yet they
have some admiration for it. Such as most despise
and spite godliness, when they are in imminent
danger of death, will readily acknowledge its excellence, and that incomparably beyond all the
fleeting honors, fading pleasures, and uncertain
riches of the world. Then, if not before, they wish
that they were godly, and they desire with Balaam to
die the death of the righteous. Numbers 23:10: "Let
me die the death of the righteous, and let my last
end be like his." They would give ten thousand
worlds, if they could, that they might be numbered
among the godly at the last day. The excellency of
God, then, should provoke you to endeavor to attain
it.

MOTIVE 2. Consider the necessity of godliness.
It is absolutely and indispensably necessary. It is not
necessary that you should be wealthy, but it is necessary that you should be godly; it is not necessary that
you should be great, but it is necessary that you
should be good; it is not necessary that you should
be satisfied, but it is necessary that your hearts
should be purified. All of you must be godly: young
and old, high and low, rich and poor, ministers and
people. You must all be godly for yourselves. The oil
of the wise virgins will not serve the foolish, and the

godliness of others will do you no good at the last day if you do not have it yourselves. What good will it do you to see godly ministers, and other godly Christians, enter into the kingdom of heaven, and you thrust out and cast down into hell?

Godliness is necessary by virtue of the precept. God commands it and God expects it. The whole course of obedience is included in the precept of godliness. If you do not obey Him in this, you will obey Him in nothing. Nothing will be accepted by God but what proceeds from a sanctified principle, this principle of godliness.

Godliness is a necessary means of avoiding eternal misery and attaining eternal happiness. Though godliness is not the cause of salvation, yet it always accompanies salvation; and though none are pardoned and delivered from the wrath to come because of it (this is only through the merits of Christ), yet none are pardoned and saved without it. Godliness indeed does not purchase heaven, yet it does lead to heaven, there being no other way to life and glory but through the narrow path of godliness (Matthew 7:14). And without holiness, none shall be admitted to the sight of God (Hebrews 12:14).

Sinners, you must be godly or you will be damned; you will be burned, and that in the unquenchable flames of hell. The fire which will burn the world will be dreadful to you if you are found ungodly; but the fire of hell which will burn your persons everlastingly will be more dreadful. The broad way of ungodliness leads to destruction (Matthew 7:13). The wages of sin is death (Romans 6:23)—not only temporal death, but also eternal.

Sinners, stay a little and think where you are running so fast: you are tumbling quickly downhill. Oh, think and assure yourselves that the bottomless pit of hell lies at the foot of the hill of sin! You are swimming along the stream of sinful lusts and affections. Oh, think where this stream will carry you, even to the ocean of God's wrath; and ere long it will certainly let you fall into those burning streams of fire and brimstone which the breath of God will kindle, and which no art or power of men or devils will ever be able to extinguish. If you do not deny ungodliness and worldly lusts, and attain unto true godliness, devils may as soon come out of hell and break the everlasting chains of darkness with which God has bound them, as you may avoid and escape those everlasting torments which, with them, God has prepared for you in hell.

And what do you think now? Is godliness not necessary? Water is no more necessary to quench fire, food and clothes are not more necessary to keep from starving, than godliness is necessary to keep from everlasting burnings, and those future miseries which no tongue can express the dreadfulness of.

Moreover, if you would be happy, you must be godly; if you would please God here, and if you would see and enjoy God hereafter in glory, you must of necessity be holy and religious. There is a crown and robes, and a weight of glory prepared in heaven; there are mansions and treasures, and overflowing rivers of inconceivable joys and pleasures at the right hand of God. But these are prepared for those who are godly. Let the necessity of godliness then prevail with you to endeavor after it.

MOTIVE 3. Consider the usefulness of godliness. Godliness is useful unto all persons: it is useful to magistrates that they may rule well; it is useful unto ministers that they may preach well; it is useful unto people that they may hear and pray and live well. Godliness is useful for all things, having promise of the life that now is and that which is to come (1 Timothy 4:8). All the promises of the covenant of temporal, spiritual, and eternal good things; all the privileges of the gospel, election, justification, adoption, free access unto the throne of grace, the guard of angels; the teachings and assistance of the Spirit, a title to the heavenly inheritance and the like— they all belong to the godly, and to none but the godly. Godliness is useful at all times: in prosperity to ballast the heart so that you may not be puffed up; in adversity to bear up the heart so that you may not be cast down; in fullness so that you may not forget God; in want so that you may not distrust Him; in life so that you may attain the end of life, namely the glorifying of God; and at death so that you may attain the end of faith, namely the enjoyment of God.

MOTIVE 4. Consider the peace of godliness. Psalm 119:165: "Great peace have they which love thy law, and nothing shall offend them." Such are godly indeed who love God's law, upon whose hearts the law is written, who love and delight in the law of God after the inner man (Romans 7:22). And such have great peace: they have peace with God; their sins are forgiven them, and, instead of God's displeasure, they have an interest in His favor and love, which is ten thousand times better than life itself; they have peace in their own consciences, at least the foundation of that peace which surpasses all understanding (Philippians 4:7). When the godly have tribulation in the world, they have peace in Christ (John 16:33). When they are persecuted and afflicted, yet they are not offended like hypocrites; neither is their peace disturbed thereby. Ungodly persons may have a carnal security; hypocrites may have a false peace; but only such as are truly godly have a true, well-grounded peace.

MOTIVE 5. Consider the sweetness of godliness. There is no true, solid comfort to be found in the breasts of any living unless it is in those who are sincerely religious. Others may have carnal joy; they alone have spiritual. Others may have earthly joy; they alone have heavenly. Others may have joy in the creatures; they alone have joy in the Lord. The joy of the wicked is sensual, brutish, devilish, short, flashy, thin, empty, and goes off with a bitter reflection; but the joy of the godly is pure, solid, durable, leaves a sweet relish behind it, and is the beginning of eternal joy. There is no such sweetness and delight to be found as that which the godly have in the light of God's countenance, the sense of God's love, the influence of God's Spirit, communion with God in His ordinances here, and the hopes of enjoying God in His kingdom hereafter. The godly alone have the joys of the Holy Ghost, which are unspeakable and full of glory (Romans 14:17; 1 Peter 1:8).

MOTIVE 6. Consider the possibility of attaining godliness. If it were impossible to get it, you might be discouraged in your endeavors after it; but as you must have it, so you may have it. Some who are as mean and vile as any of you have attained it, and why may not you? You are called to it; you have offers of it; you have opportunities for getting it; and, let me tell you, if you sincerely desire it and diligently seek after it, you shall certainly attain unto it. So much for the motives.

The next thing is to give you directions to guide and help you in your endeavors after godliness.

DIRECTION 1. Examine yourselves concerning your spiritual state. 2 Corinthians 13:5: "Examine yourselves whether ye be in the faith; prove your own selves." If you mistake your state, and apprehend that you are in the faith and have a principle of godliness within you when you are indeed in a state of nature and unbelief, nothing is more likely to effectually hinder the attaining of it. Godliness does not come by propagation, nor by education, nor by imputations, but by infusion; it is not a work of nature, but a work of God's Spirit. You may have godly parents, and yet yourselves be ungodly; you may have your nature restrained and yet not have your nature changed; you may have many moral virtues and make a profession of religion, and yet be without saving grace and true godliness. There are many nominal Christians who are not real Christians; many Christians who have a form of godliness but are without the power of it. Examine, therefore, and prove your own selves. Such are godly as have a principle of grace and spiritual life infused into them by the Spirit of God in their regeneration (John 3:3–6; 5:21, 25). Such as are non-conformists to the world and its sinful practices are transformed after the image of God in their hearts and affections, and are reformed in their lives and conversations (Romans 12:2). If you are such as the Apostle describes in Ephesians 2:1–3, "who are dead in sins and trespasses, who walk according to the course of the world, according to the prince of the power of the air, the spirit that worketh in the children of disobedience, having your conversation in the lusts of the flesh, fulfilling the desire of the flesh and of the mind"; or such as are described in Titus 3:3, who are "foolish, disobedient, deceived, serving divers lusts and pleasures, living in malice and envy"; or if you are in any other course of wickedness—you may know assuredly that for the present you are ungodly. The first step to the attainment of godliness is a clear and thorough conviction that you are without godliness.

DIRECTION 2. Labor for a sense of the danger of ungodliness. While you are ungodly, you are in continual danger of unavoidable, unspeakable, unsupportable and eternal ruin and destruction in hell. No condemned malefactor is in more danger of being hanged than you while ungodly, who are condemned to burn in everlasting fire (John 3:18; Mark 9:43–44). If death seizes upon you while you are ungodly, you are lost irrecoverably. Oh, think seriously and often that death pursues you every day; that death may be very near, even ready to knock at your door. The next meat which you eat may breed a disease within you which shall soon put a conclusion to your days. The next time you go forth from your doors, some sudden and unexpected casualty may befall you and quickly cut asunder the thread of your lives. The next sin you commit may be the finishing sin which shall bring forth death (James 1:15). And then think that your bodies shall no sooner be conveyed by your friends into the grave than your souls, having received their doom from God, shall be dragged by devils unto the bottomless pit of hell. Labor for an awakened spirit through sense of your danger while you are in an unconverted state.

DIRECTION 3. Get a sense of sin, not only as it is likely to bring ruin upon you, but also as it is displeasing and dishonorable unto God. Think while you are ungodly that you sin in everything you do, yea, you do nothing else *but* sin against God; for whatever actions do not proceed from a sanctified principle must be transgressions. Think how highly God is offended with sin; think of the nature of your sins, the number of your sins, and the aggravations of your sins; think how your hearts have been defiled with your lusts, and how God has been dishonored; think of the majesty, power, justice, and holiness of God, whom by your sins you have affronted, and let this cause you to fear. Think of the mercy, grace, goodness, and loving-kindness of God, whom you have displeased by your sins, and let this cause you to grieve. I would advise you to call yourselves to account for your sins, so far as you can remember, and make a catalogue of your sins with all their heinous circumstances. You may do it, if it is convenient, with your pens, at least in your mind; and then spread the black catalogue before the Lord in humble confessions, begging that He would work your hearts unto godly sorrow, that God would break your heart for them and from them.

DIRECTION 4. Labor for a sense of your need of Christ not only to deliver you from the guilt of sin, but also to deliver you from the power of it; not only to save you, but also to sanctify you. Be sensible of your need not only of Christ's imputed righteousness, that you may be pardoned and accepted as perfectly righteous, but also of His imparted righteousness, that you may be made, in some measure, inherently righteous. Look upon Christ not only as the example and pattern of godliness, but also as the root and spring of it; be persuaded of the truth, and endeavor fully to understand the meaning of Colossians 1:19: "It hath pleased the Father that in Him all fullness should dwell."

There is not only a fullness of sufficiency in Christ for Himself, but also fullness of redundancy for us. He is a full, overflowing, and everflowing Fountain of all sorts of supplies for us. Be persuaded that there is not only fullness of merit in Christ for your justification, but also that there is fullness of spirit and grace in Christ for our sanctification. Be persuaded that all spiritual light and life is derived from Jesus Christ. Ephesians 5:14: "Awake, thou that sleepest, and arise from the dead, and Christ shall give thee light." John 5:21: "The Son quickeneth whom He will."

Be persuaded that it is only through faith in Christ that you can have an interest in Christ, and share in any of those benefits which He has purchased or conveys; that it is through faith in Christ not only that the person is justified, but also that the heart is purified (Acts 15:9). Be sensible, then, of your need of Christ, and your need also of faith to join unto Christ that you may be quickened and renewed by Him.

DIRECTION 5. Acquaint yourselves well with the promises of the covenant of grace, and particularly those of renovation, of putting a new principle into us, of God's working the first grace. Jeremiah 31:33: "This is the covenant that I will make with the house of Israel; after those days, saith the Lord, I will put My law in their inward parts, and write it in their hearts." Ezekiel 36:25–27: "Then will I sprinkle clean water upon you, and you shall be clean; from all your filthiness and all your idols will I cleanse you. A new heart also will I give you, and a new spirit will I put within you, and I will take away the stony heart out of your flesh and give you a heart of flesh. And I will put My Spirit within you, and cause you to walk in My statutes, and ye shall keep My judgments and do them."

Such as are ungodly may have encouragement to come unto Christ and lay hold of His righteousness whereby the ungodly are justified (Romans 4:5). And such as are graceless may have encouragement to come unto God through Christ and lay hold of the promise of working the first grace, of giving a new heart, whereby they may be regenerated; and though you cannot do this by yourselves, yet in your endeavor it is that the Lord, by His Spirit, works.

DIRECTION 6. With your application of the promises of the covenant which God has made through Christ on His part, you must give yourselves up in covenant unto God on your part. Make choice of God for your God and Father; of Christ for your

Advocate and Savior, your Lord and Husband; of the Spirit for your Sanctifier and Comforter; of the Word for the rule of your faith and life; of heaven for your treasure and portion forever; and dedicate yourselves fully and freely, body and soul, unto the use and service of the Lord, resolving in the strength of the Lord to live no longer to yourselves, nor to fulfill the desires of your flesh, but to live to and glorify God with your bodies and spirits, which are God's (Romans 6:13; 1 Corinthians 6:20).

DIRECTION 7. If you would attain this principle of godliness, have no more intimate fellowship with your former ungodly companions, but associate yourselves with those who fear the Lord. 2 Corinthians 6:17: "Wherefore come out from among them and be ye separate, and touch not the unclean thing, and I will receive you." Psalm 119:63: I am a companion of them that fear Thee, and of them that keep Thy precepts." Ungodly companions will be enticing you to continue in or return to your former ungodly practices; but the godly will be persuading and encouraging you—by their arguments, their examples, and their experiences—to come into the ways of God.

DIRECTION 8. Attend upon the preaching of the Word, which is an ordinance of God's appointment and institution to work grace in the hearts of the ungodly (1 Corinthians 1:21). While ministers are scattering the seed of the Word, God may cast the seed of grace into your hearts. You may bring dark minds to a sermon, and there have them enlightened; you may bring hard hearts, and there have them softened; you may come to the Word under the

power of sin and Satan, and there be rescued and delivered, and by the power of the Spirit with the Word
have a gracious change wrought in you.

DIRECTION 9. Apply yourselves unto God in
prayer, and that every day. Confess your sins and cry
for pardoning mercy and renewing grace, and take
no denials. Though you cannot pray as well as you
would, yet pray as well as you can, and as God shall
enable you in your endeavors. Though at first you
cannot pray with grace, pray for it, and that God
would give you a spirit of grace and supplication;
and when you feel the Spirit moving, do not quench
Him, but be ready to close with His motions.

DIRECTION 10. In the use of all means to attain
godliness, use your utmost diligence. Luke 13:24:
"Strive to enter in at the strait gate." Yield not to the
indisposition and opposition of your own hearts;
hearken not unto Satan's temptations; watch, wrestle, fight, take heaven by storm.

DIRECTION 11. And last, whatever you do, let it
be without any further delay. Look upon the present
time as the acceptable time, and this day as the day
of salvation. The time past is gone and irrecover-
able; the future time is uncertain; the morrow may
never come to you; you may be in eternity before you
are a day older. Therefore, today, while it is still
called today, hearken unto God's voice; accept God's
Son; entertain God's Spirit; break off your sins and
deliver yourselves up to the obedience of the gospel;
and do not harden your hearts any longer though
the deceitfulness of sin (Hebrews 3:13).

The second branch of the exhortation is: having attained the principle of godliness, live in the practice of godliness. "Exercise yourselves unto godliness" (1 Timothy 4:7). "Live godly in this present world" (Titus 2:12). Let your godliness show itself in all holy conversation, as the text says. And here I will show you wherein you must practice godliness, add some motives, and, last, conclude all with a few directions.

QUESTION. Wherein must we practice godliness?

ANSWER. This must be done in regard to the duties of God's immediate worship, in regard to your works of mercy, in regard to your natural actions, in regard to your recreations, and in regard to the works of your particular callings.

In regard to the duties of God's immediate worship, you must practice godliness in your worshipping God more publicly in the assemblies of God's people; more privately in your families and more secretly in your closets; in the exercise of all moral virtues, in all conditions, places, companies, times, and in all relations.

You must practice godliness in your public worship, in your right use of and attendance upon public ordinances, such as hearing the Word, prayer to God, praising God, receiving the sacraments, and the like.

1. Practice godliness in hearing the Word, which God has appointed to be the means not only of conversion, but also of edification and preparation for the heavenly inheritance. Acts 20:32: "And now, brethren, I commend you to God, and to the word of

His grace, which is able to build you up and to give you an inheritance amongst all them that are sanctified." And if you would hear the Word rightly so as to receive benefit by it, you must hear it with preparation, with reverence, with attention, with faith, with affections, and follow it with a suitable conversation.

Hear the Word with preparation. Take heed that you do not come rushing into God's presence, to hear His Word as the horse rushes into battle; that you do not come reeking with worldly and filthy affections; that you do not come dissembling and making a show of hearing without any resolution to do so; that you do not come either despising some instruments who deliver the Word because of their meanness, or magnifying and expecting too much from other instruments because of their fame and powerfulness. But take the direction of Solomon from Ecclesiastes 5:1, "Keep thy foot when thou goest into the house of God," and of the apostle in 1 Peter 2:1–2, "Wherefore laying aside all malice, guile, hypocrisies, envies, and evil speakings, as new-born babes, desire the sincere milk of the Word, that you may grow thereby." Before you come to hear, endeavor to lay aside all such thoughts and affections as may disturb you; resolve to yield obedience to whatever the Lord in His Word shall command you; look up to the Lord to assist and direct ministers in preaching to you, and to accompany His Word with His blessing, through which it will become powerful, and without which it will be ineffectual, no matter who the preacher is.

Hear the Word with reverence. Remember that it is

the Word of God, and that Word whereby you shall be judged at the last day (John 12:48). Remember that God Himself is present while you are hearing, that God who is infinitely holy and jealous as well as infinitely good and gracious; and therefore you should hear with reverence and godly fear (Hebrews 12:28–29). You should tremble at God's presence and tremble at God's Word, for unto such God looks with the most favorable eye. Isaiah 66:2: "To this man will I look, even to him that is poor, and of a contrite spirit, and trembleth at My Word."

Hear the Word with attention. Hear as for your lives, as for the life of your souls; attend as if the Lord Jesus Himself preached to you, for He indeed preaches by His Word and Spirit in His ministers, who are His ambassadors and representatives. Therefore He tells them in Luke 10:16: "He that heareth you heareth Me." While Lydia attended to the Word which was preached by Paul, the Lord opened her heart (Acts 16:14). While you are attending upon the Word, God may unlock and open your heart by His Spirit, and give you such refreshing discoveries of Himself and His love as shall fill your hearts with unspeakable joy.

Hear the Word with faith. Believe that it is in truth the Word of God, and therefore assent to all the doctrines of the Word as infallibly true; rest in the promises of the Word as infallibly sure. It is through faith that the Word effectually works grace, peace, joy, and the like in the heart. 1 Thessalonians 2:13: "For this cause thank we God without ceasing, that when ye received the Word which ye heard of us, ye received it not as the word of man, but (as it is in truth) the Word of God, which worketh effectually also in you that believe." And the Apostle gives the reason why the Word does not profit, namely because "it is not mixed with faith in them that hear it" (Hebrews 4:2).

Hear the Word with affection. See the affection David had for the Word throughout Psalm 119. In verse 82: "Mine eyes fail for Thy Word." Verse 131: "I opened my mouth and panted, for I longed for Thy commandments." Verse 20: "My soul breaketh for the longing it hath unto Thy judgments at all times." Verse 163: "Thy law do I love." Verse 159: "Consider how I love Thy precepts." Verse 97: "Oh, how I love Thy law!" Verse 167: "My soul hath kept Thy testimonies, and I love them exceedingly." Verse 16: "I will delight myself in Thy statutes." Verse 24: "Thy testimonies are my delight and my counselors." Verse 103: "How sweet are Thy words unto my taste! yea, sweether than honey to my mouth." Verse 72: "The law of Thy mouth is better to me than thousands of gold and silver." Verse 111: "Thy testimonies have I taken as a heritage forever, for they are the rejoicing of my heart." Verse 162: "I rejoice at Thy Word as one that findeth great spoil."

Labor for like affections in hearing the Word. Labor that your hearts may be warm, yea, burn within you while the Scriptures are opened unto you, as in Luke 24:32. See the danger of hearing the Word without love and suitable affection. 2 Thessalonians 2:10–12: "Because they received not the love of the truth that they may be saved, for this cause God shall send them strong delusion, that they should believe a lie, that they all might be damned, who believed not the truth but had pleasure in unrighteousness."

Follow your hearing of the Word with a suitable conversation. Be as those spoken of in Luke 8:15, "which, in an honest and good heart having heard the Word, keep it, and bring forth fruit with patience." Let your hearts be cast into the mold of the Word, and let your lives be ordered according to the rule of it. Galatians 6:16: "As many as walk according to this rule, peace be on them and mercy."

2. Practice godliness in prayer unto God, which is another chief part of the worship which is due unto God. As you are God's creatures and subjects, you ought to pray, especially as you are God's children. And it is no less your privilege than your duty, so that you may have free access through Christ unto the throne of grace (Ephesians 2:18; 3:12; Hebrews 4:16). And if you would pray rightly so as to have your prayers accepted and answered, you must pray with sincerity, with humility, with faith, with fervency, with importunity, and with perseverance, waiting upon the Lord also with patience for an answer.

Pray with sincerity. Hebrews 10:22: "Let us draw near with a true heart." Do not be like the hypocrites spoken of by our Savior in Matthew 6:5 who "pray that they may be seen of men," or as those in Matthew 23:14 who "for a pretense make long prayers." The former pray out of vainglory, and that they may receive praise from men. And our Savior tells us that "they have their reward." Of the latter, who carry on some covetous or wicked design by their prayers, He says that "they shall receive the greater damnation." Be sincere, therefore; endeavor in your prayers to approve yourselves unto God; let your design be God's glory; in your prayers, seek God's favor and grace, communion with Him, and all with a sincere respect unto His glory as well as your own truest good.

Pray with humility. "God heareth the desire of the humble" (Psalm 10:17). While God "looks upon the proud afar, He hath a respect unto the lowly" (Psalm 138:6). "Be clothed therefore with humility," as the apostle exhorts in 1 Peter 5:5, when you appear before the highest Majesty in the duty of prayer. Make confession of the sin of your nature, the sins of your hearts and lives, with humility, grief, shame, and self-abhorrence. Throw yourselves down at God's feet and loathe yourselves in His sight. With Abraham, say, "We are but dust and ashes" (Genesis 18:27). With Jacob, say, "We are not worthy of the least of all Thy mercies" (Genesis 32:10). With Job, say, "We abhor ourselves" (Job 42:6). With David, say, "So foolish were we and ignorant, even like beasts before Thee" (Psalm 73:22). With Agur, say, "We are brutish, and have not the understanding of men" (Proverbs 30:2).

Pray with faith. By faith make use of the name and mediation of Christ in your prayers unto God. John 14:13: "Whatsoever ye shall ask of the Father in My name, I will do it, that the Father may be glorified in the Son." By faith apply and urge the promises which God has made to prayer, and which God has made unto faith. Matthew 7:7: "Ask and it shall be given you, seek and ye shall find, knock and it shall be opened unto you." James 1:5–6: "If any of you lack wisdom," and the same may be said of any other grace or good thing which God has promised, "let him ask of God that giveth to all men liberally, and upbraideth not, and it shall be given unto him; but let him ask in faith." Matthew 21:22: "Whatsoever ye shall ask in prayer, believing ye shall receive." And therefore you have encouragement to draw near with full assurance of faith (Hebrews 10:22). Labor for a true understanding of the meaning of the promises, and you may accordingly, with confidence, apply and plead them at the throne of grace.

Pray with fervency. James 5:16: "The effectual, fervent prayer of a righteous man availeth much." Look to it that you are righteous through Christ's imputed and imparted righteousness, for first the person is accepted and then the service. Look to it that your prayers are fervent; the fervent prayer is the effectual and prevailing prayer. Do not let your petitions freeze, as if were, between your lips; do not provoke God to deny you by the coldness and indifference of your spirits in asking; labor to stir yourselves up into fervency if you feel your hearts to be lukewarm, and cry to God for the breathings of His Spirit to kindle and blow up your affections into a flame.

Pray with importunity. Knock importunately at the door of mercy, and resolve there to lie and cry until you have an answer. Wrestle with God at the throne of grace; hang on His arm and resolve not to let Him go without a blessing; fill your mouths with arguments, and importunately plead with Him. Plead His glory, His power, His love, His Word, His truth, His Son's blood and intercession, your need, and the like, and resolve to take no denial. And if you are not willing to be denied, you shall not be denied. Importunity will prevail when nothing else will do it. See the encouragement to importunity in three places, which would be too lengthy to recite, but I desire you to read and consider them: Luke 11:5–9 and 18:1–8; Matthew 15:22–28.

Add to your prayer perseverance. Continue in the duty against all opposition and discouragement, and wait patiently upon the Lord in the diligent use of all other means that you may, in God's time, which is the best time, and in God's way, which is the best way, and in God's measure, which is most fit for you, obtain the things for which you pray. Take the direction of the Apostle in Ephesians 6:18: "Praying always with all prayer and supplication in the Spirit, watching thereunto with all perseverance"; and the example of the prophet in Micah 7:7: "Therefore I will look unto the Lord. I will wait for the God of my salvation; my God will hear me."

3. Practice godliness in praising God. Psalm 147:1: "Praise ye the Lord, for it is good to sing praises unto our God, for it is pleasant, and praise is comely." Ephesians 5:19–20: "Speaking to yourselves in psalms and hymns and spiritual songs, singing and making melody in your hearts unto the Lord; giving thanks always for all things unto God the Father, in the name of our Lord Jesus Christ." Speak forth God's praises, mingling your prayers with thanksgivings. Philippians 4:6: "Be careful for nothing, but in everything by prayer and supplication, with thanksgiving, let your requests be made known unto God." Sing forth God's praises with psalms. Psalm 81:1–2: "Sing aloud unto God our strength; make a joyful noise. Take a psalm, and bring hither

the timbrel, the pleasant harp with the psaltery."
Show forth God's praises in your lives. 1 Peter 2:9:
"That ye should show forth the praise of Him who
hath called you out of darkness into His marvelous
light." Praise the Lord with admiration, with love,
joy, and all suitable affection; and offer up your
sacrifice of praise with the hand of faith in the
name of Christ. "Hebrews 13:15: "By Him, therefore,
let us offer the sacrifice of praise unto God continually, that is, the fruit of our lips giving thanks to
His name."

4. Practice godliness in your attendance upon
the Lord's Table, and there receive the sacrament of
the Lord's Supper. This is one great command
which the Lord left behind a little before His death:
"Do this in remembrance of Me" (1 Corinthians
11:24). And though all are not presently fit for the
Lord's Table, the bread there belonging to none but
His children, yet it is the duty of all to prepare without any delay, and so to come to this Table. The
sacrament of the Lord's Supper is an ordinance of
the closest and sweetest communion with Christ of
any other, and there many Christians can say that
they have been most enlarged and comforted.

Before you come to the Lord's Table, prepare.
1 Corinthians 11:28: "Let a man examine himself,
and so let him eat of that bread and drink of that
cup." Examine yourselves in reference to your state,
whether you are in a state of grace; and though you
have no assurance of a gracious charge, yet if you
find there is a great change in your heart and life,
and you hope it is true, though hopes are mingled
with fears, you may come and possibly gain such ev-

idences as you never had before. Examine yourselves as to your graces, your knowledge of Christ, and the nature and use of this ordinance. Examine yourselves as to your sincere desires after Christ and His righteousness, your faith to apply Christ, the sincerity and supremacy of your love, the truth and firmness of your resolutions to give yourselves up in covenant to the Lord, and for the future to dedicate yourselves wholly to His service. Examine yourselves as to your sin; search what sins your hearts are most addicted to, and labor to drag them to the cross of Christ so that they may be crucified and subdued.

Moreover, before you approach this Table, read and consider how, for whom, and for what end Christ died; and labor to get your hearts suitably affected. Be sure that you do not neglect prayer unto God, so that He will give you the wedding garment, even the white robes of His Son's righteousness; so that He would help you by His Spirit and bring your hearts into the right frame; so that you may have your affections upon the wing, and all your graces drawn forth into powerful exercise.

When you are at the Table of the Lord, take heed that your thoughts and hearts do not wander. Let the gesture of your bodies be reverent, even according to the example of the apostles at the first institution of this ordinance, when our Lord was with them, and that was the posture of sitting. But look chiefly to your hearts; let your apprehensions and affections be suitable unto the representations which you have before you; labor to discern the Lord's body that your hearts may be ravished with His beauty and love.

When you see the bread broken and the wine poured forth, think how Christ's body was broken and His blood shed, and let this affect you with inward bleeding and grief for your sins, which were the cause. When you see Christ's death represented, and think what full satisfaction He has hereby given to God's justice for your sins, and what grace and glory also He has hereby purchased, let this call forth your desires after Christ and His righteousness. Let it encourage your faith to apply Him, and the promises of pardon and life through Him; let His love draw yours forth. And since He has given Himself for you and to you, give to Him your hearts. Labor for warm love toward Him, whose love for you was hotter than fire which no water could quench; which was stronger than death, and which death itself could not extinguish. Let your love also be drawn forth unto all fellow members of the same body, of which Christ is the Head. Let your love express itself in joy, and your joy in thankfulness, and your thankfulness in your self-dedication.

After you come from the table of the Lord—if in looking back upon the carriage of your heart you find it has been quite out of frame, straitened, hard, cold, and keeping God at a distance—labor to find out the cause. Surely it has been some sin, either of omission or commission. Having found it, mourn for it; make confession of it; be earnest in prayer for pardon; resolve in the strength of the Lord to take more pains in preparation against the next time, and to wait still upon the Lord until He is found. For the present, make fresh application of the death of Jesus Christ, and by later pains you may attain the benefit by the sacrament after receiving it which you could not attain in the actual receiving.

If your heart has been in a good frame, melted, warmed, enlarged, refreshed, and near God, labor to retain the sense and relish of this sweetness as long as you can. Be exceedingly thankful to God for the kind expression of His love. Be watchful against pride, resting in enlargements and all temptations to sin with which the devil will eagerly urge you. Be more frequent and fervent in prayer; draw virtue and strength from Christ's death to mortify corruption and resist temptations. Walk more closely with God; keep covenant; live up to your obligations; long for another opportunity of coming to the Lord's Table. Especially long for the second coming of Christ, when He will receive you into His Father's house to eat and drink with Him at His table in His kingdom, where you shall fully enjoy Him and eternally be with Him. So much concerning the practice of godliness in public worship.

5. You must also practice godliness in worshipping God privately in your families. You who are masters and governors of families, whatever profession of religion you make, if you do not practice godliness in your houses and set up the worship of God in your families, your profession is vain. The Lord expresses His confidence concerning Abraham's family worship as a thing which He required and was well-pleasing to Him. Genesis 18:19: "I know him that he will command his children and his household after him, and they shall keep the way of the Lord." And the command is expressed in Deuteronomy 6:6–7: "And these words which I shall

command thee this day shall be in thine heart; and thou shalt teach them diligently unto thy children, and thou shalt talk of them when thou sittest in thine house, and when thou liest down, and when thou risest up." And fathers are required in Ephesians 6:4 to bring up their children in the nurture and admonition of the Lord.

You who are masters of families, instruct your children and servants in the principles of religion; teach them their catechisms. By teaching others, you may the better learn yourselves. Read some portion of Scripture every day in your families; pray in your families with them and for them. Remember what God threatened in Jeremiah 10:25, that He would "pour out His fury on the families which call not on His name." I know some will be ready to excuse themselves with their inability to pray; but if you pray in secret, look up to the Lord for His help, study your sins and wants and the Word of God, and accustom yourselves to praying by degrees, you will gain expertise, and the Lord will give you assistance. Why should your families be like the families of heathens? And you who are under government in families, be willing to join in family worship; be diligent in learning, and ready to give an account of the principles of religion, and what you remember of the Word you have heard.

Practice godliness in your secret worship of God. Retire every day from all company into some secret place, and there look into the secret corners of your heart; search for sin so that you may confess it and be fortified against it; search for grace so that you may attain some evidence of its truth; be thankful for it and thereby be strengthened in it. Look into the

Word and search the Scriptures so that you may understand the secrets of God's will. Meditate in secret upon God's works and words. And be sure you keep a constant and daily course of secret prayer; pour out your hearts before the Lord in secret every day. Matthew 6:6: "But thou, when thou prayest, enter into thy closet, and when thou hast shut thy door, pray to thy Father which is in secret, and thy Father which seeth in secret Himself shall reward thee openly."

6. Practice godliness in regard to your works of mercy. James 1:27: "Pure religion and undefiled before God and the Father is this, to visit the fatherless and the widows in their affliction." Whatever show there is of worshipping God, and of zeal for the purest worship; whatever pretense of faith in Jesus Christ, and of love for God—yet, if there are no works of mercy, if there is no pitying and helping of others in misery, I dare affirm there is no true godliness. Neither your faith nor love is true, and it is impossible that such should attain salvation. The apostle is plain and express in James 2:14–17: "What doth it profit, my brethren, though a man say he hath faith, and have not works? Can faith save him? If a brother or sister be naked, and destitute of daily food, and one of you say unto them, 'Depart in peace, be ye warmed and filled,' notwithstanding you give them not those things which are needful to the body, what doth it profit? Even so faith, if it have not works, is dead, being alone." And the Apostle John tells us in 1 John 3:17: "Whoso hath this world's goods, and seeth his brother hath need, and shutteth up his bowels of compassion from him,

how dwelleth the love of God in him?" So that
without works of mercy, as your pretense of faith and
love does not profit others, so neither will it profit
you. See the threatening in James 2:13: "He shall
have judgment without mercy that hath shown no
mercy." And our Savior at His appearance to judgment will particularly sentence those to everlasting
fire who do not relieve Him in His distressed members (Matthew 25:40–41). Therefore, practice godliness in works of mercy.

And this you must do with simplicity and a sincere respect unto God's glory. Romans 12:8: "Let
him that giveth do it with simplicity." What you do
in this area, let it not be with ostentation and out of
vainglory. Take the direction of our Savior in
Matthew 6:1–4: "Take heed that ye do not your alms
before men to be seen of them, otherwise ye have no
reward of your Father which is in heaven. Therefore
when thou doest thine alms, do not sound a trumpet
before thee as the hypocrites, that they may have
glory of men; verily I say they have their reward. But
let not thy left hand know what thy right hand
doeth, that thine alms may be in secret, and thy
Father which seeth in secret Himself shall reward
thee openly." Let your alms be as secret as may be,
for the most part, except when by more openness
you may be an example unto and quicken others.
Always have a single aim at God's glory, so that
when you allow others to see your good works, it may
be that they may glorify your Father who is in
heaven (Matthew 5:16).

Show mercy with compassion. Pity others who are in
an afflicted condition as if you yourselves were in

their condition, especially those who are fellow members of the same mystical body. Hebrews 13:3: "Remember them which are in bonds as bound with them, and them which suffer adversity as being yourselves also in the body." Do not be rough towards the poor, and embitter to them that which you give by your insulting and upbraiding language; but be kind and tender-hearted to them, as well as liberal and open-handed. Colossians 3:12: "Put on, as the elect of God, bowels of mercy."

Show mercy with cheerfulness. Romans 12:8: "He that showeth mercy, let him do it with cheerfulness." 2 Corinthians 9:7: "Every man, according as he hath purposed in his own heart, so let him give, not grudgingly or of necessity; for God loveth a cheerful giver."

Look upon yourselves as but stewards of the Lord, that the Lord is the supreme owner of all that you have, and to Him you must give an account. What you can spare, give that to the poor, especially the distressed members of Christ as their due; you are bound by virtue of your Master's command to give to them. Yea, you ought to be denying yourselves those superfluities when many of Christ's members lack necessities. Look upon it as a privilege to have ability and opportunity to relieve others who lack, and if you have a heart to do it, this is a more unspeakable gift to you than what you contribute to the poor is to them (2 Corinthians 9:10). And this is because what you thus lay out, you lap up; you will find the return of it when all that you have besides has taken the wing, and is fled out of your sight. Therefore let this quicken you to sow bounti-

fully if you desire to reap bountifully (2 Corinthians
9:6). The reward promised is most sure, and more
than a thousandfold.

7. Practice godliness in regard to your natural actions: in your eating, drinking, sleeping, and the
use of any creature comforts. Do not be like the
horse or the swine that have no reason; do not be
like sensual, luxurious sinners who are more brutish
than those who have no religion. But let godliness
have an influence even upon those actions; regulate
your affections in your use of everything which is
the object of sense. Take heed of inordinate desires
after these things; let religion restrain the extrava-
gance of your sensual appetites, and subdue the inordinate workings of your carnal affections. You
may eat and drink and the like for necessity, and
sometimes for delight; but take heed of exceeding
the bounds; take heed that you do nothing simply to
gratify your lusts; take heed that in the use of these
things you do not abuse them, and yourselves by
them, and hereby dishonor God. What you do, let it
be by rule; and let the rule be God's Word, and let
your end be God's glory according to what was said
by the Apostle in 1 Corinthians 10:31: "Whether
therefore ye eat and drink, or whatsoever ye do, do
all to the glory of God."

Practice godliness in regard to your recreations.
That you may do this, you must make sure that your
recreations, whether of body or mind, are such as
are lawful in themselves, of a good report, and
inoffensive to the majority of sober Christians.
Therefore, forbear being either actors or spectators
of stage plays; do not be present at cock fights or

bear baitings; forbear cards and gambling. And in those recreations that are lawful, take heed of spending too much time. Take heed that they do not steal away any of that love and delight which belongs to God. Make use of them with a sincere respect to the glory of God so that, your bodies being exercised or your minds refreshed by them, you may be more fitted for God's service.

8. Practice godliness in regard to the works of your particular callings: in your buying, selling, all your commerce with one another, and the particular ways you have of gaining your livelihood. Let your godliness show itself even in those actions. Take heed that you do not engage in any unlawful calling; or, if you are engaged in such, leave it and trust God to find you another. And if your calling is lawful, look upon yourselves as called to such a way of living by God's providence; look up to Him for His presence and blessing; observe the directions of His Word as to how you might manage yourselves in your calling. As in everything else, do what you do out of obedience to God's command and with an eye to God's glory. Be diligent and industrious in your calling, and take heed of loitering and idleness. Proverbs 10:4: "The diligent hand maketh rich," but idleness brings poverty and want (Proverbs 6:9–11).

Yet do not crowd up your time so full with your particular calling so as not to reserve time for your general calling. Take time every day for worshipping God in your families and in secret. And if other works have more of your time, yet let these have most of your hearts. Be faithful in your promises; let your word be as sure as your bond; take heed of rash promises, but, having made them, if the thing is lawful and later proves inconvenient and detrimental, do not break them, for that will prove a greater detriment. Be just in giving everyone his due, and righteous both in regard to distributive and communicative justice. Do not withhold wages from any who have done you service. See James 5:4: "Behold, the hire of the laborers which have reaped your fields, which is of you kept back by fraud, crieth; and the cries are entered into the ears of the Lord of sabaoths."

Do not defraud any in your selling by light weights, short measures, or exacting unreasonable prices. Be sure the unrighteous shall not inherit the kingdom of God (1 Corinthians 6:9). "The scant measures and deceitful weights are abominable unto God" (Micah 6:10–11). And the Lord has threatened to be "avenged on all such as go beyond or defraud their brethren in any matter" (1 Thessalonians 4:6).

Take heed of all manner of collusion, deceit, underhanded dealing, or any cunning craftiness of fleshly wisdom to circumvent others and enrich yourselves; for all such gains will prove loss in the conclusion. Therefore use all simplicity, plain-heartedness, sincerity, openness, and honest, upright dealing which will yield that peace and rejoicing that all the riches in the world cannot purchase. 2 Corinthians 1:12: "Our rejoicing is this, the testimony of our conscience, that in simplicity and godly sincerity, not with fleshly wisdom, but by the grace of God we have had our conversation in the world."

9. Practice godliness in the exercise of all moral virtues which, proceeding from a sanctified principle, are graces and parts of true godliness. I shall briefly give examples of a few of these:

Be humble and modest in your deportment among men. "Put on humbleness of mind" (Colossians 3:12). "Be clothed with humility" (1 Peter 5:5). Humility is a garment which will greatly adorn you and cover many infirmities. Think and speak lowly of yourselves; if you excel in anything, do not vaunt and boast; do not be puffed up, but give God all the glory. And be so well acquainted with your own infirmities that you do not lift yourselves above others. Rather, as Romans 12:10 says, "In honor prefer others." The Apostle exhorts in Philippians 2:3–5: "Let nothing be done through strife and vainglory, but in lowliness of mind let each esteem others better than themselves. Look not everyone to his own things, but everyone also to the things of others. Let this mind be in you as was in Christ." Be not proudly obstinate and self-willed, but be ready to yield and submit one to another. Ephesians 5:21: "Submitting yourselves one to another in the fear of God." 1 Peter 5:5: "All of you be subject one to another."

Be of a meek and quiet spirit, that great companion of humility. This is such an ornament, and of so great a price (1 Peter 3:4). Refrain from anger, and endeavor what you can, especially in your own cause, to keep passion down, whatever your provocation may be. Spend your anger upon your sins, and reserve it to mingle with your love in your own zeal for God's glory; but in your own cause be meek. It is a noble spirit that can bear a slight and affront, a reproach and reviling, and not break forth into anger. Learn from Christ, who was "meek and lowly, and you shall find rest for your souls" (Matthew 11:29). Look to Christ's meekness and gentleness (2 Corinthians 10:11), who "when He was reviled, reviled not again" (1 Peter 2:23). Imitate Him, "not rendering evil for evil, nor railing for railing, but contrariwise blessing" (1 Peter 3:9). "Be not overcome by evil, but overcome evil with good" (Romans 12:21). If anger breaks forth ere you are aware, call it in again as soon as may be. "Let not the sun go down upon your wrath" (Ephesians 4:26). Read and practice what follows in verse 31: "Let all bitterness and wrath, and anger, and clamor, and evil speaking be put away from you, with all malice."

Have cordial love one to another. Live in unity and concord one with another; be tender-hearted; be friendly, ingenious, affably kind and courteous. I will give several examples: be ready to oblige all with offices of love; show kindness unto everyone as it lies in your way; be not morose and rugged, but of a sweet, winning, and courteous behavior; take heed of thinking and believing evil; forbear evil surmises and putting the worst construction upon the actions of others; take heed of speaking evil or doing evil to anyone. Romans 12:9–10: "Let love be without dissimulation. Abhor that which is evil; be kindly affectioned one to another with brotherly love." Philippians 2:1–2: "If there be therefore any consolation in Christ, if any comfort of love, if any fellowship of the Spirit, if any bowels and mercies, fulfill ye my joy, that ye be like-minded, having the same love, of one accord, of one mind." 1 Peter 3:8: "Finally, be ye all of one mind, having compassion one toward another; love as brethren, be pitiful, be courteous." 1 Corinthians 13:5–7: "Charity thinketh no evil, believeth all things, hopeth all things." Titus 3:1–2: "Be ready for every good work; speak evil of no man." Philippians 2:15: "Be blameless and harmless." If you are injured by others, be patient and ready to forgive. Ephesians 4:2: "Forbear one another in love." Colossians 3:12–13: "Put on long-suffering, forbearing one another, and forgiving one another, even as Christ hath forgiven you." Remember that if you do not forgive others, neither will God forgive you (Matthew 6:15), but will deliver you to the tormentors (Matthew 18:34–35).

Be temperate and chaste. Take heed of gluttony, drunkenness, adultery, and all kinds of luxury. Romans 13:13: "Walk honestly as in the day, not in rioting and drunkenness, not in chambering and wantonness." Luke 21:34: "Take heed to yourselves, lest at any time your hearts be overcharged with surfeiting and drunkenness, and so that day come upon you unawares." 1 Thessalonians 4:3–5: "This is the will of God, even your sanctification, that ye should abstain from fornication; that every one of you should know how to possess his vessel in sanctification and honor, not in the lusts of concupiscence as the Gentiles, who know not God." Refrain not only from grosser acts of uncleanness, but also unchaste speeches and behavior, unchaste looks and desires. Matthew 5:28: "Whosoever looketh upon a woman to lust after her hath committed adultery with her already in his heart." Practice self-denial; curb and restrain your sensual and sinful desires.

Manage all your affairs, both civil and spiritual, with Christian wisdom and prudence. Matthew 10:16: "Be ye wise as serpents." Foresee evils and avoid them, not so much the evil of suffering here, but the evil of sin and Satan's snares, and of suffering eternal vengeance hereafter, and let your wisdom and prudence show itself chiefly in your endeavors to avoid the evil of sin here so that hereafter you may escape the greatest evil, that of misery.

Exercise Christian fortitude and magnanimity. Be stout and courageous for the Lord, boldly making profession of Christ and His cause, His truths and ways, no matter what discountenance, discouragement, opposition and persecution you may meet with in the world.

Moreover, practice godliness in every condition, being content with that which God has alloted to you and sees best for you. Philippians 4:11: "I have learned in whatsoever state I am, therewith to be content." Practice godliness in every place and company; not only where the godly are present who will approve and commend you, but also in the company of the ungodly who will reproach and oppose you. As you should endeavor to encourage and quicken, to build up and strengthen those who are inside the body of Christ, so you must also endeavor, by seasonable instructions, wise and faithful reproofs, wholesome admonitions and counsels, loving and pathetic persuasions, to bring the ways of God to those who are outside the body of Christ.

Practice godliness also at all times. Be religious everyday; especially sanctify the Sabbath, spending it wholly in public and private exercises of religion, except for the time that works of necessity and mercy call for.

Practice godliness in every relationship, filling them up with the duties required in the Word. See Ephesians 5:21–6:10; Colossians 3:18–4:1; 1 Timothy 6:1–6; 1 Peter 2:13–21 and 3:1–8. Read these and then practice your duties.

As briefly as I conveniently could, I have shown you wherein you must practice godliness.

The next thing is to add some motives to quicken you to this practice of godliness.

MOTIVE 1. Consider the possibility of it. The apprehension of impossibility discourages all endeavor; but you may attain to this practice of godliness. Indeed, it is impossible to fulfill the whole law, yet, notwithstanding infirmities, you may live in the practice of godliness according to evangelical rules. You may "walk so as to please God" (1 Thessalonians 4:1). You may walk so as not to fall into any gross sin, so as to be sincerely, though not perfectly, holy in all manner of conversation (1 Peter 1:15). Indeed, you cannot do this in your own strength, but you may do it in Christ's strength (Philippians 4:13).

MOTIVE 2. Consider the necessity of it. As the principle of godliness is necessary, so also is the practice of it for you to escape eternal misery and attain eternal happiness.

MOTIVE 3. Consider the difficulty of it. It is no easy thing to practice godliness, to walk in this narrow path out of the common road of the world, to be upright and maintain integrity, to be blameless and harmless, the children of God without rebuke in the

midst of a crooked and perverse generation
(Philippians 2:15). It is no easy thing to keep your
light shining when there are so many winds of tem-
ptation about you to puff it out, and such floods of
corruption within you to extinguish it. You will find
it difficult to follow Christ, bearing His cross; to
deny yourselves, to thwart your carnal interest, to
mortify the deeds of the body, to strive for passage
through the strait gate, to stand continually upon
your guard, to fight the good fight of faith. All this
and more is included in the practice of godliness;
but the difficulty should not discourage you, but stir
you up to more diligence in your endeavors because
of the necessity and possibility of it—yea, because of
the readiness of the Lord by His Spirit to help and
make that easy for you which is so difficult for flesh
and blood.

MOTIVE 4. Consider the glory of it. The practice
of godliness brings glory to God: hereby you will
glorify your heavenly Father in the eyes of those who
behold you. It brings glory to Christ: hereby you will
appear to be His disciples, and show forth the virtue
of His death and intercession. It brings glory to the
Spirit: hereby it will appear that the Spirit of God
dwells and works in you, making you differ from all
others in the world. It brings glory to your profession: hereby you will adorn the gospel and make the
profession of it glorious which is so often spoken
evil of through the scandalous lives of some professors. It brings glory to yourselves: God will honor
you; good men will esteem you; and this will also put
a luster upon you in the eyes of the wicked.

MOTIVE 5. Consider the utility or profitableness

of it. By your practice of godliness, you will be profitable unto others. You will be a blessing in the places where you live; you will be like pillars to the building, like stakes to the hedge. This will also bring in the best gain for yourselves.

The practice of godliness will bring you to the truest gain, such riches as are solid and substantial, such as shall yield you true satisfaction, not like the windy and empty things of the world.

It will bring the clearest gain, that which is the greatest, and withal the cheapest, though it cost Christ dearly. You shall have it for nothing, for the acceptance of it. While the gain of worldlings costs them their souls, your gain shall be clear; and with the gain of grace you shall gain salvation.

It will bring the surest gain, that which shall be beyond the reach of men and devils, or death, to deprive you of.

It will bring the sweetest gain; such peace, delight, and joy shall you find in the strict service of God as all the pleasures of sin are not worthy to be mentioned with.

And at length it will bring eternal gain. It will bring you to the possession of the heavenly inheritance which is incorruptible and incomparable.

The last thing is to leave you with some directions to help you in the practice of godliness. I am forced to be brief.

DIRECTION 1. Be sure you attain the principle of godliness in your regeneration; otherwise there can be no practice of godliness. This I have spoken to at length already.

DIRECTION 2. Acquaint yourselves well with the rule of godliness, which is the Word of God; read, study, and apply the Scriptures.

DIRECTION 3. Apply yourselves by faith every day unto Christ, the Fountain of godliness. Draw virtue and strength from Him for the performance of duties, the resisting of temptations, the bearing of afflictions, and to enable you in the universal exercise of godliness.

DIRECTION 4. Be much in prayer unto God, and especially for His Spirit to guide and assist you in this godly practice.

DIRECTION 5. Endeavor to remove all impediments to a godly course and conversation. Remove those distempers of mind within you and forbear those things which may be an occasion of sin outside you.

DIRECTION 6. Make use of all the helps and furtherances of godliness which God puts into your hands, such as good company, good books, and God's ordinances.

DIRECTION 7. Be often comparing your heart and life with the rule of the Word. Get your conscience enlightened, and set it to work. Hearken to it and take heed of offending and wounding it.

DIRECTION 8. Be very watchful. Keep your hearts with all diligence. Guard your senses; make a covenant with your eyes; take heed what goes forth from the door of your lips and what comes in the door of your ears; walk circumspectly.

DIRECTION 9. Lay before you the patterns of Christ's conversation when He was here on the earth, and also the example of good men. Be followers of Christ, and of men so far as they follow Christ.

DIRECTION 10. Set yourselves under God's all-seeing eye continually. Remember that a holy and jealous God is always with you, that He compasses your path and your lying down, and is acquainted with all your ways (Psalm 139:3).

DIRECTION 11. Labor for a deep impression of the last things, namely death, judgment, heaven, and hell. The frequent consideration and due impression of this upon your minds will exceedingly help, and will quicken you in the exercise of godliness.